THE
DANCE
OF THE
DOLPHIN

Also by Karyn D. Kedar

God Whispers:
Stories of the Soul, Lessons of the Heart
(Jewish Lights)

THE DANCE OF THE DOLPHIN

finding prayer, perspective and meaning in the stories of our lives

KARYN D. KEDAR

For People of All Faiths, All Backgrounds

JEWISH LIGHTS Publishing

Woodstock, Vermont

The Dance of the Dolphin:
Finding Prayer, Perspective and Meaning in the Stories of Our Lives

Library of Congress Cataloging-in-Publication Data
Kedar, Karyn D., 1957–
    The dance of the dolphin : finding prayer, perspective and meaning in the stories of our lives / Karyn D. Kedar.
        p. cm.
    ISBN 1-58023-154-3 (Hardcover)
    1. Spiritual life—Judaism. 2. Prayer—Judaism. 3. Kedar, Karyn D., 1957–
    —Anecdotes. 4. Life—Religious aspects. 5. Jewish meditations. I. Title.
    BM723 .K346 2001
    296.4'5–dc21
                                                                    2001003246

10   9   8   7   6   5   4   3   2   1

Manufactured in the United States of America

For People of All Faiths, All Backgrounds
Published by Jewish Lights Publishing
A Division of LongHill Partners, Inc.
Sunset Farm Offices, Route 4, P.O. Box 237
Woodstock, VT 05091
Tel: (802) 457-4000   Fax: (802) 457-4004

www.jewishlights.com

To Talia, Shiri, and Ilan—my children

My teachers of poetry, song, and sweetness

CONTENTS

Meaning

ACKNOWLEDGMENTS

To my husband, Ezra, and three children, Talia, Shiri, and Ilan, you are my teachers and the joy of my life. I promise I'll make dinner again, soon. To my parents, without the foundation of kindness, love, and enthusiasm you give so freely, I think I may have periodically gone mad.

To my writing circle, Steve Yastrow, David Gottlieb, Betsy Katz, and Lisa Fisher, for the creative synergy; writing is hard and lonely, and you all make it less so. To the Skokie Boulevard Lunch Club for hours of conversation, music, and mutual support. To the children who are watching us closely, Talia, Nurit, and Ari, Shiri, Levi, and Jonah, Ilan, and Noah. Pursue your passion, cultivate your creative energy, and never take no for an answer. You are loved.

To my spiritual guide, Carol Dovi, thank you.

To the Yastrow family. *Mi casa es su casa,* or was it the opposite? To Steve, for a constant exchange of ideas, creative passion, and a sense of frenetic urgency. To Arna, for intelligent calm, perspective, and gentle (most of the time) reminders of what is important to me.

To Mimi Dunitz, for laughter—always, no matter what, who, and where, laughter. You remind me that the sacred need not be serious. To Ellen and Sherry, for noticing and tending to the details. They say that God is in the details.

To Nan Goldberg, my editor, for her careful reading of the images and words. To Emily Wichland, managing editor at Jewish

Lights, for her compassionate intelligence and kind professional-ism. To the wonderful people at Jewish Lights for their encourage-ment and dedication to the mission of bringing light to the world. Thank you to Stuart M. Matlins, publisher of Jewish Lights, for backing his vision with the drive to make his dream a reality.

May the Eternal Spirit of the Universe always pursue me with that annoying itch that pushes me out of complacent thought and lazy habit. May the Divine Creator of All always nurture me with creative musings and holy encounters. I accept the paradox that has become my life with gratitude.

IMAGING THE DANCE

I have never seen a dolphin on the open seas. I've been to various aquariums and many a sophisticated aquarium, where dolphins splash and click as they perform tricks to delight the children. But that's not what I mean. I have never seen a dolphin on the open seas as she swims and dives and flirts, arching her body with a gentle superiority. Someday I will; I dream of it all the time. I imagine it will go something like this:

We are on a boat for what seems like a long time. The bright sun throws sparks and splashes of light against the tips of the waves. Perhaps a spray of seawater carrying one of those sparks stings my sunburned lips. Just as I bring a bottle of fresh water to my mouth, I pause slightly and squint into the distance. I can't tell where the water ends and the heavens begin. It is as if an artist, painting in oil pastels, used her thumb to smudge all distinctions on the canvas. Eternity, I think, must reside in a blurred line of blue. Suddenly the boat tilts with a wave, and close to its flank is the most beautiful creature I have ever seen. She lifts and arches out of the water and then submerges again. I gasp, holding my breath, holding the moment. All I can say is "Did you see that? Did you see that?"

I have never seen that moment, but I have named it. I call it "the dance of the dolphin." It is a dance that is both beautiful and essential. It has grace and eloquence.

The dolphin dances because to survive she must live simultaneously in two elements that are seemingly incompatible. She must live in both water and air, and she must dance between the two.

She dances because she is commanded to from the moment of her creation. She dances because her instincts are pure genius and they are the source of her survival. She dances, and as she does, we watch in awe, every time, never tiring of the spectacle. She dances, and we learn.

We learn that we too must live in two elements that are seemingly incompatible. We must live in the rational world while earning a living, making a name for ourselves, providing for our loved ones, our feet planted firmly on the ground so as not to stumble. And yet it seems we must also live in the world of the spirit, finding our center, searching for meaning, giving without regard for receiving, reaching beyond reason, creating, while not tripping on the ground beneath our feet. We should never lose the feeling in our souls. And to survive, to live with joy and a sense of calm and purpose, we must dance between the two.

We must learn the dance because life at its best is the seamless integration of all aspects of self: worlds seen and worlds experienced, the world of doing and the world of being. We must dance between our physical needs and spiritual needs because the human experience demands that we eat and that we be nourished. We must sharpen the rational faculty and strengthen the intuitive. We must be strong and yielding, protecting and vulnerable. Life, at its greatest, is like the dolphin's dance. It possesses beauty, power, and grace.

The dance is an arch between contradictions.

We have been taught the laws of the rational world, to believe what is physical and logical, to distrust what is unseen, inconclusive, illusive. We have been encouraged to think, to analyze, to accomplish, to make as much money as possible, to read a good book, to place a napkin on our lap. We have learned to be socially acceptable, to get along, to reach for success. Rarely are we encouraged to yearn, to dream, to recognize our passion, to live our passion, to rely on our intuition. Seldom does a parent whisper into the heart of a child that he is a creative, beautiful being made in the image of God. It takes courage, skill, and self-reliance not to fear the unfamiliar language of the Great Mystery. Have we learned to decipher its code?

In 1973 I had a dream that stunned me. I was studying Hebrew on a kibbutz in an intensive class, which was designed to immerse us in the language during classroom study, work in the fields and factories, and our social time with our Israeli friends. Every waking hour we heard Hebrew and were urged to speak it.

For me, the study was difficult and tedious. My days and nights were filled with grammatical rules, awkward sentence structure, limited vocabulary, and simple thoughts. Until one night. It must have been about four months into the seven-month program when it happened. I had a dream entirely in Hebrew. I woke up excited and ran to tell my friends that I had crossed the river to compe-tence; I had reached a new plateau. They shared in my excitement and asked me what the dream was about. I stared backed at them speechless; I realized that I'd had an entire dream in Hebrew and I hadn't understood one word of it. Did you understand it at the time? my friends asked. I don't remember, I answered. Skeptical, they turned away, and we went to class.

The dance immerses us in the language of two worlds. Just as the ordinary matters of life require a language, so does the extra-ordinary world. We must develop a vocabulary that expresses won-der, engages our fears, describes our sense of holiness, and whispers God's name in all the richness we yearn to experience. The dance will help us become fluent. When I wake and while I sleep, whether I am feeling sharp or weary and bored, as I dream and as I envision, I want to understand as best I humanly can.

Like the dolphin, we have been commanded to dance from the very moment of our creation. We begin with Adam and Eve (or Chava, as she is called in Hebrew). They live in a story that establishes essential archetypes. Adam and Chava are warned not to touch the Tree of Knowledge, the Tree of Life. The tree is pleasant, and it is in the middle of the garden. Three questions tickle the rational mind: If they are not to eat from the tree, why create the tree at all? And if creating it, why make it pleasant to see? And if making it pleasant, why place it in the middle of the garden?

This is what I call the ultimate set-up, the "wet paint theory" at work. There is a bright red shiny bench in the middle of a park, with a sign on it that says "Wet Paint." Most people see the sign and touch the bench. Adam and Chava were not exceptional; they were us. In this Garden of gardens, the beautiful tree in the middle, the tree whose fruit contains all essential knowledge and whose juice is life itself, is created as a set-up for what transpires.

"Touch the fruit and you shall surely die." They touch, they eat, and they live. They live but they are punished, or so it seems at first glance. Adam must work the land and Chava must bear children.

But it is here that the dance begins. Adam must work the earth; his name in Hebrew means "earth." Chava must bear children, and in Hebrew her name means "life." They do not die; instead they live to become who they were always intended to be. Adam symbolizes for us an essential grounding, sustenance, bread from the earth, fruit of the vine. He is the symbol of all that is physical and necessary. Chava symbolizes the life force, creativity, regeneration. These are the primary functions of the spirit. We know that inside us is life eternal, renewing itself like the very act of creation. The core of who we are is divine, and therefore we possess a light and life whose nature is creative, giving, and loving.

We tell the story of Adam and Chava around the hearth; in the faces of our children we see light play with shadow, and we yearn to live the archetypes. Life offers a fruit-bearing tree, the opportunity to partake of its wisdom, the ability to become who we were intended to be, the need to live between the physical and the metaphysical. You rise to the occasion of yourself.

Like the dolphin, we have been commanded to dance from the very moment of our creation. And as it is with her, we dance because our instincts are pure genius and our wisdom is the source of our survival.

We must learn the dance, which instructs the rational and inspires the spiritual. We must count our money, build our homes, consider our deeds, and, above all, measure the moments that draw us closer to love. It is the dance that is important. As far as I can tell, there is nothing we know absolutely—not God, not the geology of the Rocky Mountains, not the reason for fear and pain. But I can dance as I strive to understand and experience it all; I can dance, spreading my arms toward what is seen and what is unseen, what is actualized and what is merely imagined, between the physics of a star and the poetry of a pinpoint of light against the black heavens. I can ride the light of knowledge and inspiration. "Hitch your wagon to a star," Emerson wrote. Indeed. That would get us somewhere.

And so we begin to examine the dance by considering three paths, three different languages, if you will: prayer, perspective, and the journey toward meaning. All three can synchronize the rhythm of our heart with the way of the world.

Prayer is the process through which our soul connects with the Divine, with all that transcends our being. It enables us to converse with things invisible, forming connections that at times defy the rational but often calm the spirit. It can be the language that tickles and soothes, itches and scratches, touches ever so gently the soft spots deep within. Prayer, like words or even complicated mathematical formulas, is a language to be mastered. And in doing so, we open gates that are usually closed and often locked.

Perspective is among the most powerful tools the rational mind possesses. Worlds rise and fall based on the way we choose to see events, rationalize experience, or process information. Perspective is a choice. We take in the data of the world, process it for meaning, and use it to support a certain point of view or perspective.

We can choose how we define life's twists and turns and, in choosing, define the very quality of our lives.

Lastly, we walk the narrow path that leads us to the grandest of dance floors. It is the path toward meaning, where the urge to understand and make sense of it all—that push or internal stirring—is itself the path. We yearn to reconcile all that seems incompatible. There is an urgent need to listen to God's heartbeat, to make sure events are happening for a reason. I search for the bridge that will connect life's contradictions to a greater good.

Prayer, perspective, meaning: The dance of the dolphin.

PRAYER:
THE LANGUAGE OF
THE SPIRIT

PRAYER

In the simple swaying of the heart in song and poetry,
In the yearning to reach beyond the walls of self,
I find the moment
Where I have stretched every muscle of my soul
And my fingertips touch the boundaries of heaven.
It is a healthy longing to dance with the Divine.

In a silent scream of terror caught in my throat,
Where a grunt barely audible is stifled,
As I try to breathe through my suffering,
In the exclamation point of sadness, of confusion, of wonder,
I find the perpetual question of the spirit.

So

I pray alone or I pray with others.
I pray though I am sure no one is listening.
I pray because I am sure that my prayers are heard.

In the hissing of the midnight wind,
In the flapping of the wings returning home from the south,
In the empty stare of dismay and
In the wrinkles of my eyes as I smile,
O God, hear.

THE IRON WINGS

In the moments before my eyes opened, the morning deceived me. The smell of the air, the quality of the sunlight, the birds, the sense of peace all transplanted me from a suburb in northeast Illinois to Hod HaSharon, Israel. In the mid-eighties, the Hod, as we called it, was a dusty village. It had no traffic lights, only stop signs. It had no supermarket, only small, crowded Mom and Pop stores, one every couple of blocks, where you paid for milk and fresh rolls by signing an index card at the owner's cash register. Instead of a sidewalk, it had a long dusty dirt path that connected it to the next village, which was called Magdiel. It was a path I walked at least twice daily. I lived in the Hod and I worked in Magdiel and my sandled feet were always dirty.

The Hod was famous for two things. First, if you traveled from Haifa to Jerusalem, it was a bus stop for those who lived in one of the nearby cities that clustered together to form Israel's belly. Second, and perhaps most important, it was in serious competition for the site of the best falafel in the country. On the side of the road, right near the busy bus stop, was a wooden hut about the size of a small backyard shed. It was painted vibrant blue, lest you miss it. Inside the hut stood one man; there was only room for one. Without moving his feet, with the mere twist of his waist and wrist, he formed falafel balls from the batter, placed them in the vat of boiling oil behind him, and scooped them out into fresh pita stuffed with chopped salad and tehina.

He moved so quickly, so gracefully, with such concentration and focus, that often I found myself standing at a short distance, watching him as if I had discovered a street dancer bound for greatness. The bus stop was always busy, and there was always a crowd huddled around the hut, waiting for their manna. The word *manna* was used in the Book of Exodus for the sweet sustenance that fell from heaven as the Israelites wandered in the desert; today it means a portion of food, or, in slang, a falafel with pita. I passed this hut at least twice daily on my trek from the Hod to Magdiel and back again.

Once, I was in a hurry to get to work and I didn't pause to watch the falafel man and his devotees. I rushed past to the dirt road, but when I was a distance away, something made me turn around. There it was, the vibrant blue hut in the distance, with a thin line of smoke rising from the cooking falafel, giving off the most delectable aroma. As I stood fixed in the dirt between Magdiel and the Hod watching the hut and its cult, I saw the smoke rising first toward the sandy foothills of the coastal plains, then to the Judean Mountains, then to the heavens to an unsuspecting God.

Suddenly, I pictured the sacrificial cult of the early Israelites who offered incense to God just fifty miles southeast of there in Jerusalem at the Holy Temple. *Ketorit*, they called it. Worship in those days involved all the senses: smell, touch, taste, hearing, and, of course, sight. I envisioned the devoted group, huddled around the altar to a God they could only imagine, a people sure that this invisible God would enjoy the sensations of this world—otherwise, what's a world for? Worship was physical, it was messy, and it had everything to do with the life you lived. It involved the best the agrarian life had to offer. The best fruit, wine, grain, livestock, the best effort. Worship was gratitude for life and its abundance.

We don't pray like that any more. We do not offer up the entrails of bulls, the broken-necked turtledoves, the libations of wine, and alas, no incense offerings. Most of us are just as happy to read about the days of sacrifice, relegating it to the category of "what we used to do, but no longer." Instead we pray from books in sanctuaries and occasionally alone.

But too often our prayers are sterile, primitive, or stillborn. They are sterile when they are the rote response of a prescribed tradition. They are dull when they lack the emotional commitment and physical labor of the pilgrim who walked one hundred miles to offer his first fruits at Jerusalem's Temple. They are primitive when they are yet another transaction we perform: If You do this, I will do that. They are stillborn when they lack the spiritual and intellectual energy that gives life to the things we hold dear.

Sylvia Plath writes this criticism of poetry:

These poems do not live; it's a sad diagnosis.
They grew their toes and fingers well enough,
Their little foreheads bulged with concentration.
If they missed out on walking about like people
It wasn't for any lack of mother love.

O I cannot understand what happened to them!
They are proper in shape and number and every part.
They sit so nicely in the pickling fluid!
They smile and smile and smile and smile at me.
And still the lungs won't fill and the heart won't start.

They are not pigs, they are not even fish,
Though they have a piggy and a fishy air—
It would be better if they were alive, and that's what they were.

But they are dead, and their mother near dead with distraction,
And they stupidly stare, and do not speak of her.[1]

Our prayers do not suffer from bad composition, nor do they lack wisdom and healing power. When they lack life, it is because we have not infused them with energy and vitality. They contain all they need to fly, and yet "the lungs won't fill and the heart won't start," because we, who pray, merely sit and rise on command, read and are silent at the appropriate moments, politely listen to music and sermons. We have become passive. "They are dead, and their mother near dead with distraction, and they stupidly stare, and do not speak of her." To speak of Her, of God, we must act as if prayer is an activity, a dance, a song, a communal and private journey through time and inner space. The ancient ones had it right: prayer is physical as well as spiritual, and it involves commitment greater than simply filling a pew.

This story is not new, however. It is not simply a sign of the times that prayer, spiritual poetry, and song are absent despite the attempts at reading the words. Meyer Levin tells a story handed down from the disciples of Rabbi Israel, known as the Baal Shem Tov. He lived in the Carpathian Mountains during the seventeenth century. Levin begins the tale in this way:

> The Enemy did not forswear the battle, but came out openly and spread his iron wings between the earth and heaven. The wings were as thick as the mountain is high, and all through they were made of heavy iron. He wrapped his wings around the earth as he would enclose it within the cups of his hand.
>
> On the earth, all was darkness. The wings of the Enemy pressed forever closer to the earth, and crushed the spirits of men.
>
> When Rabbi Israel was about to enter into a synagogue, he stopped outside the door and said, "I cannot go in. There is no room for me to enter."
>
> But the Chassidim said, "There are not many people in the synagogue."
>
> "The house is filled from the ground to the roof with prayers!" said the Master.
>
> But as he saw the Chassidim take great pride because of his words, he said, "Those prayers are all dead prayers. They have no strength to fly to heaven. They are crushed, they lie one on top of the other, the house is filled with them."[2]

What is the Enemy that envelops our world with iron wings and prevents our prayerful ascent to God? What causes our world to be darkened and our souls to be heavy and sluggish? We feel superior to those who lived in the days of sacrifice. But then, the masses walked on foot and the rich brought donkeys, and they traveled from the ends of the known world, Babylonia and Egypt, to "go up" to Jerusalem and offer their best produce and livestock. They walked for days, carrying, lugging, leaving behind. Does the word *sacrifice* apply to their burnt offering or to the calluses on their sandled dirty feet?

Hannah Senesh lived during a dark time, when the enemy of all that was good in humanity was closing in fast. She had emigrated from Hungary in 1939 to settle on a kibbutz in Israel; however, her life was not destined to be lived as a simple poet-farmer. In 1943, she joined the Palmach, the Jewish army in Palestine. She became a paratrooper and was the only woman chosen to be part of an elite unit whose mission would bring her behind enemy lines in Hungary in the midst of the Nazi invasion. The unit successfully retrieved vital information for the Allies and aided Jews in their escape.

Hannah was captured, tortured, and beaten beyond recognition. Yet she did not reveal to the enemy the radio code, which would have harmed the Allies. She died at the hands of her anti-Semitic countrymen.

One day, before she was called to be a heroine, before she joined the army, before she knew her fate was not to be a poet-farmer, Hannah was walking on the beach, not too far from Hod HaSharon. She was overcome by the perfection of it all, feeling the sand of a million years between her toes, and she wrote the following prayer:

My God
I pray that these things never end
The sand and the sea
The rush of the waters
The crash of the heavens
The prayer of the heart.

The prayer—or poem, as she probably would have preferred—is so simple that it may seem trite to our modern sensibilities, and yet, how true are her words. So many of us blame the Evil One for our lack of faith or our inability to connect through prayer. But Hannah Senesh did not succumb to evil. For Hannah, prayer and simplicity were the same. "May these things never end," she wrote. Simply that. "May the rush of the waters and the crash of the heavens" never end. May our prayers never end. The language of the spirit speaks in the simplest terms. It is a language that hears the music of the world and the beat of the heart as one. It is a language that senses what is true and right in muted sounds and wispy images.

Simplicity is a lost human trait.

And yet it was simplicity with which Rabbi Israel sought to pierce the wings of the Enemy. The story continues that one day a young boy who was known to be "slow-witted" came to Rabbi Israel's synagogue for the high holidays. He brought with him a flute that he had made from a reed. During the prayers he became restless, for he was unable to read the Hebrew and participate. During the last prayer of the holiday when all were on their feet, the boy could no longer contain himself and took the flute from his pocket,

> set it in his mouth, and began to play his music. A silence of terror fell upon the congregation. Aghast, they looked upon the boy; their backs cringed, as if they waited instantly for the walls to fall upon them. But a flood of joy came over the countenance of Rabbi Israel. He raised his spread palms over the boy David. "The cloud is pierced and broken!" cried the Master of the Name, "and evil is scattered from the face of the earth."[3]

Who is the Enemy that envelops our world? Perhaps a modernity that values complexity and tolerates complacency. Truth need not be complicated, and complacency must never be tolerated.

How dare we live in a world where cynicism rather than curiosity guards our souls like soldiers of the iron-winged Evil One? Perhaps we cannot pray because for a century or so we have been taught not to. It is illogical to pray.

Indeed it is. Faith, God, and prayer are suspect, for they cannot be measured or easily understood. So we of faith have gone underground. As a civilization, we have forgotten how to open the soul. The irony is that we have not abandoned our sanctuaries entirely. We sit there quietly, politely, rather bored, not quite getting it. Our prayers are deadened by our minds.

To pray, we must relearn how to sacrifice. Not the animal sacrifice of the ancient days but a sacrifice of self or, even better, of self-consciousness. It is not silly to loosen your thoughts in moments of wonder. It helps you leave the prison of self-obsession and enables you to connect with the universe in its most basic and pure state: the sand, the sea, the rush of the waters, the crash of the heavens.

The words of others, the words of your heart, silence—all are not only legitimate but are necessary steps toward reconnecting with the world in a way that will ultimately bring you peace. Simplicity is what we need: the ability to spontaneously call a moment beautiful, like the smoke rising from a blue hut at the crossroads of a village town, or the crush of pilgrims at Jerusalem's gate, or the sound of the waves against the shore. These are prayers that pierce the iron wings of the Enemy.

You seek forgiveness, then seek the most basic prayer there is: God, teach me to know, feel, and live the beauty of life.

Say this every day until you know that it is true, and then say it every day thereafter, so we all may learn.

———

I met the boy in Baal Shem Tov's story at a camp in Wisconsin one cold and rainy summer. We were praying: I, the rabbi; they, the teenagers. Our prayers had been rather weak, dampened by routine, exhaustion, and sore throats. Adam volunteered to read a prayer. A few days before he had told us that he had attention deficit disorder and was taking medication for his condition. Indeed, Adam was different, keeping to himself, prone to outbursts, never really looking me in the eye. But this morning, he volunteered to read.

He began, pausing after every word as if to check himself for accuracy. In fact, every so often he became stuck, like we all did when we began to read. When his pauses grew a bit too long, I would help him by saying the words for him: "struggles and strivings," "companionship," "confusion," "uncomplaining," "loneliness," "exult," "toil." He would repeat after me and we formed a rhythm, slow, steady, together.

As he quietly read on, laboring, glowing with a true and earned sincerity, my heart opened up, aching for all those who suffer the pain and gift of being so clearly different. I felt a tenderness for this boy, for the countless boys and girls whose lives are a struggle. I remembered the pain of my own youth. I heard his halting prayer and my heart soared, piercing the iron wings. With a lowered gaze, he gently and ever so sweetly brought the prayer book to his lips and kissed a corner of the cover. I felt as if his lips had touched my soul. He had led us in prayer.

I turned to him and thanked him for finding the dead prayers. I told him that I had prayed, really prayed, for the first time in a long while. Though we were finished, I opened to the page that Adam had conquered. I told the rest of the group that they should not take for granted what came easily. That many of us, many of them, struggled, that God was with them in their struggle. I began to read once again the prayer he had opened with:

> Lord, You give meaning to our hopes, to our struggles and our
> strivings. Without You we are lost, our lives empty. And so
> when all else fails us, we turn to You! In the stillness of the
> night, when the outer darkness enters the soul; in the press of

the crowd, when we walk alone though yearning for companionship; and when in agony we are bystanders to our confusion, we look to You for hope and peace.

Lord, we do not ask for a life of ease, for happiness without alloy. Instead we ask You to teach us to be uncomplaining and unafraid. In our darkness help us to find Your light, and in our loneliness to discover the many spirits akin to our own. Give us strength to face life with hope and courage, that even from its discords and conflicts we may draw blessing. Make us understand that life calls us not merely to enjoy the richness of the earth, but to exult in the heights attained after the toil of climbing.[4]

Dear, dear Adam, may it be true. Amen, *Selah*!

NAVIGATING THE HEAVENS

Prayer is not for the sake of external intervention but rather for the hope of internal transformation. I don't ask for miracles, flashes of light, and even good health. Prayer that supports my spirit does not ask or demand that God intervene in the flow of life but rather support me, elevate me, strengthen me against the onslaught of its waters or the stillness of its depth. I have never found that negotiation, blackmail, or temper tantrums work with matters of the spirit. I need help, grace, kindness, a sense that I am supported and not alone, no matter what happens to me in the course of things.

Author Anne Lamott writes in her book *Traveling Mercies*, "Here are the best two prayers I know: 'Help me, help me, help me,' and 'Thank you, thank you, thank you.' A woman I know says, for her morning prayer, 'Whatever,' and then for the evening, 'Oh well,' but has conceded that these prayers are more palatable for people without children."[5]

I like that. The greatest prayer of all is one of gratitude. When I can't feel grateful, I ask for help.

I hate flying on airplanes. I am absolutely sure each time I fly that it will end in disaster. I have even written eulogies for myself while on the ground waiting to take off. Then we begin to fly, and

I am sure that this time the sound isn't right, the plane is moving too slowly, the angle is off, the noise is odd. If God wanted people to fly, we would have wings. It is wrong to violate natural law and as my punishment, well, that will be that. So far, I've been wrong.

There's an unwritten code while flying during the business traveler's rush: no eye contact. Eye contact could only lead to conversation, and conversation inevitably leads to the question I most dread in these circumstances: "So, what do you do?" An honest answer to that question leads to the unwanted conversation that has only a few texts. "Oh, really, I never knew women could be rabbis." Or, "I haven't been back to temple since my bar mitzvah." Or, "You wouldn't believe what my rabbi did to me." Or, "My rabbi didn't once show up at the hospital when my mother was dying." Or, "How is it that you people do not believe in our Savior?"

So I follow the code, eyes slightly down or blankly straight ahead. Once I was on my way home from a book signing, and I settled into my seat, trying to look relaxed. It was the last flight of the day, and the plane was filled with weary business people. Trying not to break the code, I glanced at the person across the aisle from me and noticed his long legs. I remember thinking that he was probably uncomfortable; I glanced at his face to see if I was right and saw a young man in his twenties, probably in sales. He was looking straight ahead—he knew the rules.

I closed my eyes during takeoff and said my customary prayer, "God, may it be Your will that we reach our destination in peace." I repeated the phrase "May it be Your will" over and over like a hysterical mantra, until we reached altitude. Then, regaining my composure, I read to keep my mind distracted from impending danger.

We were in our "final approach into O'Hare Airport" (an unfortunate phrase) when we suddenly hit unbelievable turbulence. The plane tilted side to side and up and down with such intensity that I was sure the pilot's knuckles were as white as my face. I glanced outside to see how close we were to the ground and wondered how many miles we could plummet and still survive.

I closed my eyes and prayed in pulsating whispers for courage, for courage, for courage, for life, for courage, for the hope that eternity indeed exists, for courage, for my children, for their courage. Then I felt the weight of a large hand on my shoulder. Although I didn't open my eyes, I knew it was the hand of the young man across the aisle. The words of my prayer merged with the warmth of his touch. For what seemed like a lifetime we were still, my eyes turned toward God, his hand securely on my shoulder. Then we landed, safely.

I opened my eyes and looked into his. We smiled. He said, "I saw that you were praying, and I wanted you to know that you were not alone. I was praying too." Still shaken, I whispered, "Thank you." As we left the plane, he said to me, "So, what do you do?"

"I'm a writer," I said.

"What brought you to Ann Arbor?" he asked.

"I was at a book signing."

"What's the name of your book?" he asked.

"*God Whispers*," I answered.

Busted, as my ten-year-old daughter would say. "*God Whispers*! Man, I was praying with the right person!" We walked briskly, not speaking, no eye contact. I went to the right toward ground transportation; he went to the left toward baggage claim.

I feel his hand on my shoulder nearly every time I am scared.

Ours was a wordless prayer. The real prayer rested not in my thoughts or his but in the space between. Prayer took the form of touch, a sensation of some great hand reaching across a vast isolated space, making contact.

Prayer connects us to a transcendent power, a power beyond words or thoughts or poetic formulations. With a simple touch I met this power, and it went deeper than words to an overwhelming sensation that I am not alone.

MEDITATION ON THE BEACH OF BOCA RATON

My friend Carol has always been, well, on the cutting edge of my spiritual world. Like a sharp knife, her ideas slice away what I have thought to be true and right, revealing new layers of belief. So when Carol wants to do something, or uses a word in a new way, or wants me to read a new book or listen to a new tape, I usually pay attention. And when I don't pay attention to her, I pay attention to my resistance.

"Can I take Talia with me New Year's Day to a world meditation for peace?"

"What?" I have come to expect something like this from my friend.

"Every New Year's Day, people gather in communities throughout the world to meditate for peace. I found out that a group is gathering at the beach at 5:00 A.M., and I thought it might be nice to take Talia."

She knew not to ask me to join them. The closest I ever came to meditation was asking Carol how it went during her morning practice. I looked at my five-year-old daughter. With her silky blonde hair and almond-shaped blue eyes, she was an exotic cross between her Israeli father with Syrian ancestry and her American mother whose family was from Russia and Poland. Talia was dreamy, always off in a quiet world of play and fantasy, never quite focused on what we thought she should focus on. I liked the idea of introducing her to Carol and her ideas. "Sure," I said. "If she wants to go." They left and returned before I was even awake for the New Year. "It went fine," they said later as I sipped my late-morning coffee.

Twelve years later, my family and I were in Denver visiting Carol for the winter break. New Year's approached and Carol said, "I thought I would take Talia to the world meditation for peace, for old time's sake."

"Fine with me," I said.

Eleven-year-old Shiri chimed in, "I want to go too."

For some reason, I didn't want Shiri to go. Unlike her sister, Shiri was active, restless, friendly, easily bored, and very bubbly. Not the meditating type, I thought. I didn't want her to be restless and bother the others. But true to form, she persisted; something cool was about to happen, and Shiri was not going to be left out.

At 4:15 A.M., my girls were dressed and out the door with my friend. They came home a couple of hours later and slipped into bed to sleep a bit more. I woke up at about 8:30 and was bored, so I went into Carol's room.

"Are you awake?"

"No."

"What are you doing?"

"Sleeping."

"So how did it go? Was Shiri a problem?"

Carol lifted her head from the pillow. "She was fine. She sat for about ten minutes. Then she wrote a great poem. Then she went to the back of the room, lay down, and fell asleep."

Carol put her head down. I think she was trying to go back to sleep.

"When did you get back?" I asked. I was up; it was time for her to be up.

"The meditation was long, about an hour." Carol shifted in her bed. "When we were done," she continued, "I woke Shiri up to leave and she looked at me and said she was sorry she fell asleep but that she'd dreamt about world peace."

I smiled and sat at the edge of my friend's bed, quietly. I wondered if Shiri's dream counted in the work of universal consciousness toward creating world peace. I tried to let my thoughts float by, watching the disconnected words lightly touch my mind, my heart, and then my spirit. Carol sat up in her bed, realizing that her sleep was irreversibly disturbed, not realizing that I was truly trying to "get quiet."

"Did I ever tell you what happened twelve years ago when Talia and I went to the beach in Boca to meditate?"

"No," I said, still watching the disconnected words take form and vanish into the air around us.

"Well, we all sat on the beach facing the ocean. It was dark, but you could tell the sun was about to rise. I told Talia that she could sit with us but if she needed to get up, maybe she could collect shells."

I had the image of my blonde little girl running on the beach searching for treasure while tens of adults sat still in silence, with their eyes closed, facing the waves.

"When we were done," Carol continued, "I asked her how she did. She had filled the fold of her sundress with different-shaped shells, and her face was bright and peaceful, yet curious. She said, 'The sunrise was so beautiful, but you and your friends missed it because your eyes were closed.'"

With their eyes closed, Carol and her companions experienced the Divine Wisdom of the Universe; with her eyes open, Talia saw the Divine Wisdom of the Universe.

Many people advocate meditation instead of prayer as a vehicle for reaching this solitude and silence, believing that prayer imposes truth but meditation takes in truth or, as Deepak Chopra has been quoted as saying, when you pray, God is listening, but when you meditate, God is speaking.

Meditation is a tool, but you should enter the silence any way you can. Laurie Beth Jones has written in her book, *The Path*:

I have never been able to fully empty my mind. But I am quite capable of losing it. I lose it—or "loosen it"—whenever I am riding my horse named Desert Star out among the cotton fields. I "lose it" when I am standing in a hot, hot shower, letting the water sting and stimulate and "sensate" my back. I lose it when I sit with my mother and watch the clouds billow and mushroom and bloom over a Sedona sunset sky. I lose it when I see sunlight hitting a reed tipped by a red-winged blackbird. When I am most aware of the beauty in God's world is when I lose my mind.[6]

I long to slip into cracks of silence where breath is connected to spirit and spirit to wind and a sense of oneness resonates in my core.

GRACE

Grace. A moment in time in which you know that you are loved unconditionally by God and therefore are connected to the core of things. That there is no separation between you and all that is good and true. And so we pray: *M'halkel haim b'hesed*—God sustains the world in love, and we wait for the moment when we believe that it is true.

Grace. A moment in thought where you are not alone, for you realize that you are part of a living, breathing creation. A moment where you understand that the unfolding of your life has meaning. And so we pray: *Ahava raba ahavtanu Adonai Eloheinu*—with great abundant love we are supported by God, and we wait for the awareness that it is true.

Grace. The intertwining of thought, intention, and deed to the highest possible good. Like tiny threads of sheep's wool twisted into a single strand of yarn, stronger, more useful, brilliant. And so we pray: *Vehafta et Adonai Elohecha*—and you should love God with all your heart, with all your soul and with all your might, and we hope that what we do reflects that command.

The story is told by Hanokh of Alexandria:

> Once there was a stupid man who each morning had a difficult time remembering where he had left his clothes the night before. So one day he got a pencil and a piece of paper and wrote down where he was placing each article of clothing. He

placed the note next to his bed and thought to himself, "Tomorrow I will have no trouble finding my clothes." He awoke the next morning, quite pleased with himself, took the note and followed it to the letter, finding each piece of clothing exactly where he had set it down. Within a short period of time he was fully dressed. Suddenly he was seized with a terrible thought: "But where am I?" he cried. "Where in the world am I?" He looked everywhere but could not find himself.

"And so," taught Hanokh of Alexandria, "so it is with us."[7]

Grace is knowing your place in the world. In fact, the word for *existence*, the word for *place*, and one of the names of God, *Maqom*, are all derived from the same root. *Maqom* is the moment you know that the place in which you live is a place both physical and metaphysical. This *maqom*, place, is a location and yet transcends locale; it is both now and forever, both apparent and invisible. *Maqom* is where purpose and place are one. When you know that, even for a split second, you are in a moment of grace.

I knew that early one Sunday morning while sitting on my dining room floor with my son staring at the wall.

It all started with a redecorating scheme, which involved removing the yellow wallpaper with strawberries that was in my kitchen and the Chinese pattern that was in my dining room. I was going to paint the kitchen a pale blue and the dining room white except for one of the walls. I wanted to paint one of the dining room walls a deep blue. People said the dining room was too small, the color too dark; the pale-green chairs wouldn't match. But I could not let go of the thought of a blue wall in my dining room.

For me the color blue has always been the essence of spirit. Perhaps I associate that color with the vastness of the sky, the reach toward the heavens, or maybe I connect it with the power and mystery of the sea. It just seems that everything blue in nature signals us to notice some divine greatness.

I wanted one deep-blue wall in my dining room, the place where friends and family meet, where we assemble to obey the command of hospitality and form a sense of lasting community. The dining room can be a holy place, the table an altar for good food, Torah study, sincere conversation, song and laughter. One wall just had to be deep, deep blue. So when my Israeli painter added his voice to the naysayers—"You shud paint de vall vhite, it's cleen and brings light to da rrroom"—I flashed back to the whitewashed walls in my Jerusalem apartment and found my resolve. I looked him square in the eye and said, "We're going to paint it deep blue. And another thing—make it high gloss."

So he did. And I am in awe. No pictures on this wall, just blue.

On my wall I can imagine a world with no horizon, just a blended line between the heavens and the earth that is indistinguishable. Sky and sea are one. In front of the wall are the chairs, the color of sea foam, empty as if waiting to be filled by some mysterious guest named Elijah. And the table: long, square, flat, inviting you to lean, learn, feel welcomed.

I didn't know it at first, but with the blue wall I was inviting moments of grace.

And so it began one morning in the early fall. The sun hit the high gloss with a slanting splash of light, illuminating thoughts as deep as the blue. I stared at the wall and felt that place and purpose are one, that I am witness to harmony right in my own dining room. All converge—godly love, home, family, wish and dream, light and blue. Grace.

I was in the habit of waking early on Sunday mornings before I taught a class to enter a sort of meditative space. I would wander to the bookcase that used to be my grandparents' and now holds the books that inspire me, pull out a volume or two, and think. I never really organized those books into specific categories or put them back in the same place, so that when I reached for something, its neighbor would often create some irony or paradox, like the *Rubaiyat* of Omar Khayyam next to the Bible.

This particular Sunday, I made a cup of coffee and pulled out a collection of poetry by Rainer Maria Rilke along with Martin Buber's Hassidic stories. On my way to the bookcase I had caught a glimpse of the early-morning sun on the blue wall and was about to go to the dining room to read, think, stare, and drink my freshly brewed coffee, when I looked up and saw Ilan, our nine-year-old son, standing on the stairs. His eyes were the color of dream. He was warm and soft and still smelled like sleep.

I took his small hand in mine and said, "Ilan, come, I want to show you something." We went down the stairs and rounded the corner and there it was: the high-gloss blue wall splashed with sunlight. "Look, Ilan, isn't it beautiful?" He said in a hoarse early-morning voice, barely audible, "Yeah." There we sat, in the dining room, in front of the wall, on the cold Pergo floor, legs crossed, cuddling, staring, breathing in unison.

A moment of grace.

Annie Dillard writes, "In any instant the sacred may wipe you with its finger."[8]

AND THEN THERE WAS LIGHT

For Deborah Sue Maheshi Smith z"l

We were in Garden City, New York. Nearly one hundred women from the Women's Rabbinic Network assembled to pray, study, and consider matters of mutual concern. For many of us, the prayer services at these conferences are the most transforming moments: women's voices united in song and intention, pushing the tradition to new boundaries, creating moments of safety and sanctity, sharing holiness, lost in the depths of our own lives. These moments are joyful, tearful, intensely personal, and refreshingly communal.

In the hotel ballroom where we prayed, there was a chandelier that was made up of long rectangular pieces of crystal several feet long, at least a hundred of them in each fixture. They were close together, and the light source was somewhere in its core. These crystals would gently sway as we prayed, and I would think to myself, they are moving because of the forced air that circulates around the room. And yet I could not take my eyes off them. Where was the light source, what made them move, what were they trying to teach me?

This year's conference was good, with many moments of friendship, learning, and light.

Finally in the last session, when we sat together for one last prayer service, the swaying of the crystals became my focus once again. I was sitting next to Faith Joy, a younger colleague whom I didn't know very well. I wanted to lean over and ask her a question somewhere between the *michamocha* and the *Teffila*, "Faith, what do you think is the meaning of the chandelier? You know, the way it moves like that." But I resisted. I was afraid she would think my question bizarre, and I didn't want to intrude in her prayer.

Suddenly, during the silent meditation, as I was watching the moving light from above, I remembered another chandelier; this one was round with hundreds of small crystals as large as the entire ceiling of a good-sized ballroom.

It was in a hotel in Beverly Hills, California. It was eight years ago. I had just returned from living in Israel for seven years. My first assignment in my new job was to go to Los Angeles for a conference of Jewish educators. The first night I was there, a violent shaking awakened me. It was an earthquake. I had never been so frightened in my life. Only a few months earlier, I had experienced the Gulf War in Jerusalem, with gas masks and sealed rooms, and yet this shaking of the earth shook me to the core. The newscasters added to the fear. They were predicting the Big One.

Eventually I got dressed, and the hotel had a beautiful Sunday morning brunch with pancakes and omelets and waffles and cheeses and smoked fish with bagels and muffins with fresh whipped butter. I made my way around the buffet several times, tasting a little of each of the different foods. The omelet chef eyed me as I approached him for the second time. I said to him, "I know this is not helping in the long run, but it sure as hell is helping me in the short run." I thought I could eat my panic away.

Suddenly another aftershock. The chandeliers swayed back and forth. I said my prayers; I thought I was going to die.

My mind shifted back to Garden City. I looked at Faith Joy. Her eyes were closed, and she was deep in prayer. She had lost her sister that week and was in mourning. I looked up at the crystals and watched as they gently moved to the silence of prayer. I quietly took out a pen and notebook and wrote:

In Los Angeles the summer of '92
The chandeliers swayed from the
Earthquake that threatened the very foundations
Of my life.
In Garden City the Spring of 2001
The long rectangular crystals on the chandelier swayed
From the voices of the angels
As they said amen to our prayer.

In Los Angeles I feared for my life
In Garden City my life was filled with the awe of God.
I saw sparks dancing from above like
The flashes of light in a naughty child's eye.

I wonder which swaying rocks my soul more completely
The one from above or the one from below
The one that threatens or the one that uplifts.
The one beneath my feet or
The one that trembles as a crown of diamonds above my head.

Where is the glory of God, the angels ask?
The blessing of God's glory is in its place, they answer.

So I learn from the cracks that threaten my steps
And I learn from the cracks up above that allow
Slivers of Divine light to seep through.

This I know—
The shaking of the earth made a deep throaty rumbling noise
The shaking of the heavens was silent.

We finished our prayers, said the last amens, asked God's blessing on one another, and prepared to return to our lives. I saw Faith Joy and told her what my thoughts were when we were praying, how I wanted to know the metaphor of the chandelier but resisted the urge to ask her.

She looked at me and said, "When my sister died I was at home. My father was on the way to my house to tell me she was gone. I was upstairs and my son was downstairs. Suddenly he screamed, 'Mom, the lights, the lights!' Could it have been my sister departing this world?" I touched her shoulder and looked at the ripped black ribbon she wore to symbolize her mourning. "Yes," I said. "I think it could have been." I looked over my shoulder at the crystal chandelier. It was swaying, and the light was dancing like sparks off the tip of a wave.

MYSTERY

God is the Mystery of existence.

Enter the Mystery. Enter the Mystery not to know but rather to sense the Soul of the Universe. Enter the Mystery in order to banish the arrogant notion that all is knowable if only we were smart enough. Enter the Mystery because that's where wisdom resides, floating like the purity in air—essential, invisible to the naked eye, felt only by the naked soul.

The Mystery of life as uncertain, elusive, imperfect creation continues. We tend to want to stay away from that which we do not know; therefore we avoid the Mystery. But Mystery is always there, like air, like life itself, or like the creek behind our house. So plain, yet we deny seeing it.

Enter the Mystery. Enter slowly, softly, heart first.

The rabbis of the Talmud called the Mystery "the *Pardes*." The word *pardes*, from the Greek, is where our word "paradise" comes from. In Hebrew it has come to mean "orchard." I think of the *pardes* as an orange orchard.

I was seventeen, and a terribly sad high school graduate, when I went to the orange orchard of Kibbutz Hatzor. I once heard someone say that for the first twenty years of your life you grow up, and then for the second twenty you heal from having grown up. I went to the kibbutz, like so many in that decade, to heal from the first twenty years of growing up. We were to be volunteer farmers, helping bring in the crops. I'd rise at 4:00 A.M., a bit insulted at the hour until I stepped outside. The early morning beauty would dissolve my resentment.

There was a spot on my way to the orchard that took my breath away. I would stand on a dirt path that split into three directions. One direction led to the cotton fields and beyond them the Mediterranean Sea. In the other direction were the Judean hills climbing ever so slowly toward Jerusalem. Straight ahead was the way I was headed, to the orange orchard.

I always paused at this spot, just to breathe in the possibilities of life—they seemed so varied at that crossroads. I would then continue silently to the flatbed truck to meet my coworkers. It seemed clear to all that this was no time for words. The truck would stop at the entrance to the *pardes*. I'd pick up a burlap sack from a pile and hang it across my chest. I was ready.

When you first enter the *pardes*, you are struck by the smell. It is almost toxic. The entire universe smells like sweetness: no exhaust fumes, no morning breath, no brisket, not even the smell of fear can penetrate the heavy veil of orange that hangs in the air.

I look up, and I am utterly astounded by the sharpness of shape and color where the world is at once physical and metaphysical—Crayola® orange, green, and blue in shapes of round, oval, and vast sky. The ground is soft and a bit muddy. My boots feel each step as heavy, slow, and sure. As I pick the oranges, my burlap sack becomes heavy and my shoulder sags from the weight. And I ache from the truth of it all. Yes, the rabbis were right to call the Mystery "the *Pardes*." This is the place where beauty, truth, and meaning are as tangible as smell, color, and mud.

But Mystery, by definition, is not concrete. So the *Pardes* can be a confusing place. We cannot abide not knowing. It frightens us.

Four entered the *Pardes*, the rabbis wrote. Ben Azzai peeked at its entrance and died. Ben Zoma looked in and went mad. "The Other" lost his God. Only Rabbi Akiva left in peace.[9]

To engage in the Mystery is to befriend the unknown as a travel companion, wise and constant. This is what sustains me. We run so fast in the opposite direction, and most of us don't even know where that has taken us. Where are we now, having escaped the feared "not knowing"?

There are three types of knowledge that adults possess: I know, I used to know, and I don't know. I know that in 1492, Columbus sailed the ocean blue. I used to know that plants are green because of a process called photosyn—…something. I don't know God. Unlike some information in this category, God is simply unknowable and therefore will always be in this third category. So we don't talk God-talk.

We adults run from "I don't know." We spend a lifetime trying to know, understand, and appear reasonably smart. "I don't know" embarrasses us because for some reason we think we should know. Do you remember the year you could no longer help your child with her math homework? Third grade, fourth, eighth grade? Do you remember what you said to her? "Well, dear, it's the new math, we didn't learn it that way." Or, "Ask your father." Or, "Didn't you bring home a book?" Or, "We'll get you a tutor." Or—the ultimate attempt at avoidance—"Your teacher gives too much homework; I'll have to talk to her."

Unlike long division, God is perpetually unknowable.

Mystery is to be embraced, not avoided. It is the place where the great secrets of the universe are told. In the center of Mystery there sits, like an ancient treasure chest hidden long ago, wonder and awe. Swirling around the edges of Mystery is learning, the kind that leads to wisdom. Mystery is the magic dust that transforms the mundane into a life glittering with significance. Once you have found the courage to enter the Mystery, you are less likely to be overwhelmed with fear ever again.

COMMUNAL PRAYER: THE PHILOSOPHY OF THE MINYAN

The story is told of prayer:

> Once there was a bird that was the most magnificent creature in the world. It had a wingspan greater than anyone had ever seen. It had every color imaginable, bright blues and pinks and reds and purples. It was truly a thing of beauty. It fact, it was so beautiful that when it flew into a certain village, the king was struck with awe. Day after day he would watch this bird fly about the village and know that he was seeing the most beautiful thing in the world.
>
> One day, the king decided he wanted the bird for himself, for he knew that if he captured it he would have in his possession the most beautiful thing in the world. So the next day he ordered his villagers to capture the bird and bring it to him. The villagers wanted very much to please the king, but it seems the bird had perched atop the highest tree in town.
>
> The king, seeing their frustration, ordered them to build a human ladder in order to reach the bird. The villagers agreed, and the largest and strongest men got down on their hands and knees and ordered their neighbors to climb on their backs. And so it went, one after the other climbed onto the backs of the next until they nearly reached the top of the tree. They needed one more person, so the smallest child in the village carefully climbed up the backs and shoulders of all who

came before her until she reached the very top, right opposite the bird. The child reached for the bird and...[10]

The story has an ending. But somehow, every time I tell it I seem to forget how it goes. Even as I footnote the passage, I resist reading the last lines. There are, I suppose, many possible endings. It is possible that some guy on the bottom got bored or decided the whole thing was rather stupid, and he got up and walked away and caused the whole human ladder to come crashing down. It is possible that just as the child was about to capture the bird, it flew away. It is also possible, it seems to me, that she caught the bird.

But as the years go by and I tell this story over and over again, I have come to envision a different ending. I think that after climbing to the top on the backs of her entire community, when the little girl came face to face with beauty, and she began to reach to touch the tips of its wings, there she stayed, suspended in awe forever.

Whenever possible, that is where I'd like to be: supported by a community of strength and noble intention, in a perpetual reach, with beauty at my fingertips, suspended in awe.

In the midst of communal prayer I have been that little girl. To be suspended in awe is to be lost in the purr of song as we pray, watching the melodies climb onto the back of tradition and then reach beyond. To be suspended in awe is to have no psychology, no self-consciousness. It is to be powerless over swaying, like a field of wheat that surrenders to the wind. To be suspended in awe is indeed to be a child filled to the brim with pure delight and brilliance of soul. It is like a great yielding from the center, allowing room for the Spirit of the Universe. To be suspended in awe is to unfold and stretch out the core of whom you dream of being.

Yes, I am lost when I am praying. I am lost because I become a part of some great entity beyond myself. Community, prayer, song,

God, and I are all one. For a moment I am in suspended awe, I am lost, and I am filled. When I am transformed by prayer, it is as if I am in love.

———————

Sometime in the year 1965 or maybe 1966, I became a Jew. I was born a Jew to Jewish parents, but I think that sometime just before my tenth birthday the whole thing sank to the bottom of my soul to live there forever, sparkling like buried treasure. The light in the dining room on Friday nights had a special glow. Challah, candles, wine and nice dinner napkins formed an aggregate of light, smell, and texture. It really felt as if we were inviting the angels of Shabbat to come and bless our home. We would eat and leave for temple, always impressed with what a handsome family we were.

Temple had an air of importance to it, and I had access to the rabbi's study before services because my father was always on the board and often on the *bimah*. We always sat in the front row, up front, as close as possible. The rabbi's wife, Essie, sat one row behind us, on the aisle. When Daddy was on the *bimah*, his eyes would crinkle into kindness, he would smile, even wink, for the whole congregation to see that he loved *me*.

Much to my mother's dismay, I would play with my pretty patent leather shoes right there in the front row, taking them on and off. She would try to get me to sit still, but I wouldn't. Sometimes I would take my white gloves off, turning them inside out and back again. But as the service progressed, I would settle in close to my mother. We would hold hands. Her hands were soft with perfectly shaped, unpainted nails and pretty diamond rings and a large gold charm bracelet dangling from her wrist. But mostly I remember how soft her hands were; I would trace her fingers and rings.

If one were looking at this scene, which took place every Friday night, one might believe that this little girl was not listening, that she was bored, fidgety, that she probably belonged at home with a babysitter or at a children's service.

But I loved services, the drone of adult words and austere music that provided a background to my thoughts and daydreams. Stroking my mother's hands, I learned that "peace is our most precious gift," that I was to "love God with all your heart, all your soul, and all your might," that the "meditations of my heart should be acceptable unto God," and that "the study of Torah is equal to it all because it leads to it all."

When you pray often, prayer becomes what you know. It can serve as a textbook for your beliefs and values.

I was recently at a national conference on synagogue transformation. One of the late-night exercises asked us to reflect on our earliest Jewish memories. Many memories flashed through my mind, and I tried to do a mental chronology. Turning the years and ages around and around, trying to figure out what came first and what was next, I lost my way completely, and those early memories ceased to be particularly poignant for me. So I decided not to share.

Others in the group, however, shared beautiful recollections, and I listened and was moved. The conference continued for a couple of days and my thoughts bounced to other issues, other questions. On the way to the airport I was staring out the taxicab window at Philadelphia in a gray drizzle, wondering if there would be flight delays, when I suddenly flashed back to a childhood image.

In a cold corner of the unfinished basement of my parents' home sat a large mahogany desk that had once belonged in the law office of my grandfather, Lewis H. Schwartz, whose distinguished practice spanned sixty years. He began his practice in Lawrence, Massachusetts, just before his twentieth birthday, and stopped work a month before his death at eighty-four.

Our basement, which became home to this desk after his death, was dark, with pipes and wooden beams for the ceiling and gray cement for the floors. A single sixty-watt bulb hung from the ceiling from an electrical cord. The basement was cluttered with books and old furniture, supplies, papers, and filing cabinets, boxes of relics from a life put away for safekeeping. It was impressive and inviting down in the basement, like the smell of vintage book dust. It was a place of endless fascination and hours of play for my brother and me; in fact, it still is. Sorting through the meticulously collected stuff of people's lives is like embarking on a dusty treasure hunt, with its triumphant cries of "Mom, remember this?" or "Neil, look what I found!" or "Daddy, can I keep one of these?"

As a child, I found myself drawn to that desk time and time again. I liked its seriousness; it seemed so heavy with importance. I liked the scratches on the top of the desk, which revealed a light color beneath the dark veneer that gave a bit of texture to the flatness. I would trace them with my small finger and think of the wrinkles on an old lady's face, deep with silent and secret stories. I liked the clutter of paper clips of all sizes and sorts, the yellow legal pads, and the boxes of government-issue black ballpoint pens.

That afternoon in rainy Philadelphia, sitting in the cab on the way to the airport, I let my mind wander aimlessly through the details of this memory when, with a flash of insight, I realized that playing "meetings" was my earliest Jewish memory. My dad, an attorney for various government agencies, would always come home at six, have one Scotch on the rocks, read his mail, and quickly have dinner so that he could go to the temple for a meeting.

I was proud of this. It seemed that he was engaged with very important matters, endeavors of grave consequence. Indeed he was. He was sustaining the Jewish people in his off time, bringing God to earth, forming character in his children. It's little wonder that I played "meetings." I was emulating the aura of importance, the pursuit of meaning and purpose. In fact, it was so profound that one might say I grew up to meet for a living.

In 1957, five months before I was born, after years of thinking, formulating, considering, and collecting the right words, Martin Buber wrote a book on meetings. In the conclusion to his book *I and Thou*, he writes: "The existence of mutuality between God and man cannot be proved, just as God's existence cannot be proved. Yet he who dares to speak of it, bears witness, and calls to witness him to whom he speaks—whether the witness is now or in the future."[11] To meet, Buber believed, is an endeavor grounded in Holiness. We need only dare to speak of God and relationship begins.

We've been meeting for generations. It is written in the Book of Exodus, a book devoted to the power of wandering, "And it came to pass that anyone who sought God would go out to the Tent of Meeting."[12] With everything the Israelites needed in their desert journey, the Tent of Meeting was central. How else could they encounter the Divine Spirit unequivocally? The call was put out to the collective wanderers: The Tent of Meeting is outside the boundaries of camp. To meet God, you must simply desire such a meeting and then walk to the designated meeting place.

In fact, in the Bible the word *moed* designates a sacred place, a sacred time, and a sacred gathering. In the days of the desert wanderings, when the Israelites searched for a destination, they carried with them their *ohel moed*, their Tent of Meeting, a place where God was to be found. They convened "holy convocations" where groups of people formed a circle of holy intent.

The synagogue is a house of meeting. Its name is a direct translation into Greek from the Hebrew *bet knesset*.

To meet, it seems, has great potential.

As a child, I played "meetings," but as an adult I yearn for all kinds of meetings. I yearn for meetings of the mind, where thoughts and ideas collide in excitement as they try to find their way toward becoming reality. I search for meetings of the heart, where company and community replace isolation and loneliness. I seek meetings of the soul, where wounds are healed and pain is comforted. And I dream of meetings with the Divine: moments and places where holiness resides.

In the morning prayers, as we begin to form a minyan, the quorum required for communal prayer, we recall an ancient story in which curse turned to blessing.[13] Israel's enemies stand high on the mountaintops of Moav looking at the sand-colored valley below, hot and barren except for Israel's black tents dotting the landscape. The large tents are divided by tribe, yet pitched together as a people.

The king of Moav, Balak ben Tzpor, tries to organize a curse to destroy the Israelites, weaken their strength, send them scattering, but instead of a curse a blessing comes forth: *Mah tovu elohecha Yaacov, mishkenotecha Yisrael.* "How good are your tents, O Jacob, your dwelling places Yisrael." No matter how the king orders and commands, the curse turns to blessing. It is so incredible a possibility, that our curses should turn to blessings, that we sing this blessing every morning that we assemble to pray together.

But the mystics add another element. After counting ten for a minyan, they add a verse from Leviticus: *vehafta l'recha kamocha.* "Love your neighbor as yourself." Having counted the physical minyan, they connect as a spiritual community by acknowledging the command to love one another. Once having formed a community, both in numbers and in spiritual intent, we proceed with the morning prayers.

We are called to climb onto the backs of the community, suspended in awe, reaching for beauty. We meet under the tents of Jacob to pray, to rise above the expected, to reach beyond the limitations. The king of the village has demanded that we reach for holiness no matter how elusive, that we strive to truly understand who we are and who we are to become.

It seems that great things can happen when we meet. We need only to seek God and go out to the Place of Meeting.

MAY THE WORDS OF
MY MOUTH

I had been invited to the Lutheran School of Theology to participate on a panel about spirituality in different faith traditions. This
seemed like an interesting opportunity, and I accepted.

The panel met on a cold but sunny February morning. Following
the directions, I drove through early-morning rush hour traffic to
Hyde Park, the neighborhood of the University of Chicago. I had
trouble parking on the busy streets and it took a while until I
found a space, which was blocks away.

By now I was late. I stepped out of my car into the wind. The
sidewalks were icy, so I found myself walking quickly in the middle
of the street with the sun and cold in my face, trying to avoid the
oncoming traffic. I hadn't noticed the Lutheran School before. I
approached the oddly shaped black building and found the
entrance, where I was greeted by the organizer of the event, who
was a bit nervous that I might not arrive on time. We were minutes from beginning. I asked for water, took off my coat, and tried
to shift my thoughts from parking to Spirit.

We were ushered into a large auditorium with theater-style seat-
ing that went straight up to the second floor. The panelists and I
were on a stage below, looking up at the three hundred ministers
and theology students. I took my place between the other two panelists. To my right was the Sufi scholar. She was dressed in the traditional black garb for Muslim women, covered from head to toe.

To my left was a young Buddhist priest. He was dressed in white, a simple robe with a sash around his waist. The Sufi had brought a written text to speak from; the Buddhist had brought bells. I wore a chocolate-brown pantsuit with a coral sweater peeking out from beneath and coral lipstick to match. I had to borrow a pen.

As the moderator stood to speak, my heart began to race. I was truly stunned. Here we were together—Lutheran, Muslim, Buddhist, Jew—each with our own theologies, each with our own historical paths, all converging on this moment.

I had two thoughts. First I thought: Surely the angels are sitting up taking notice at this moment. I wondered if they were giggling or holding their breath. The second thought was: What could I possibly say, what should I say? I whispered to the world, and myself, *God, give me the words to speak to what unites us.*

But as I stood up to speak I had no words, at least none I wanted to say. So I began with a moment of silence for peace around the world. Everyone bowed their heads, and I closed my eyes. Through the silence, phrases formed in my mind, thoughts collected from their scattered places of banishment. In the silence my heart stopped pounding and started beating again. I spoke of ways in which the Jewish tradition tells us to connect with the universal Spirit of the Universe, through listening, through paying attention to the moment, through a system of actions that force us into ethical and moral relationships.

At the end of the six minutes that were allotted to me, the moderator sounded the bell he had borrowed from the Buddhist priest. The priest was next up. He taught this:

Life exists in the tension between paradoxes. It is as if you use a walking stick with two ends; only one at a time can guide your way, but as one end digs deep in the ground to stabilize your step, its opposite end is pointed to the heavens. Take faith and doubt, for example. When you are being guided by faith and your heart is filled with the greatness of all things, faith grounds and stabilizes your every step. But its opposite, doubt, is the other end of the stick, and it ironically points toward heaven. Doubt is ever with you. Even as faith is your guide, doubt is traveling with you, and with it the potential sense of alienation and insignificance. Learning, he said, takes place in the context of paradox.

He went on, but my mind lingered on the tension between paradoxes. The bell sounded, and the priest took his seat. I smiled at him and nodded at a job well done, but I knew that the walking stick was now mine in the many perpetual journeys I travel. The tension between paradoxes is where I live, it is where I learn and grow, it is what takes my breath away. I always believed that in the space between opposites, God played a kind of jump rope, going in and out, keeping a steady rhythm, always in danger of tripping.

Rainer Maria Rilke writes,

Just as the winged energy of delight
Carried you over many chasms early on,
Now raise the daringly imagined arch
Holding up the astounding bridges.

Miracle doesn't lie only in the amazing
Living through defeat of danger;
Miracles become miracles in the clear
Achievement that is earned.

To work with things is not hubris
When building the association beyond words;
Denser and denser the pattern becomes—
Being carried along is not enough.

Take your well-disciplined strengths
And stretch them between two
Opposing poles. Because inside human beings
Is where God learns.[14]

There are many paradoxes that live through us. One of the most compelling is our need to speak and our need to keep silent. They stretch out taut like pegs on the opposite sides of a tent.

Through my words, worlds are created and destroyed. I have the power to build and tear down. Twice a day I hold my son in my arms and whisper in his ear, "You are my favorite son." To which he replies, "I am your only son." To which I say, "God, I'm so lucky to have you."

But what of the son whose father shouts that he is lazy and useless? Or whose mother never says anything at all but turns her back on his need to hear her? This power to destroy cannot be underestimated.

What I say defines who I am. When I speak, the curtain is drawn open upon my dreams and fears, and my words reveal a person who is troubled, inspired, scared, and confident. The words I use, all of them, are incantations that yield great power.

But what I don't say also defines who I am—the words I don't use to stand up for someone who is oppressed, or the words I don't use to insult or criticize. I am defined by the words I don't say to reveal an injustice no one else has the courage to address. I am defined by the words I don't say when I am angry and scared. Through my silences, worlds can go on quite alone in their torture.

But there is another kind of silence. It is the one that stifles the urge to speak because in fact I should listen, watch, wait. Through my silences I have a unique power to hear and see in ways that I can't when the noises of my mouth distract. Worlds unfold and are revealed when I choose silence. All these silences, in different ways, define who I am.

On the most solemn day of the year, when Jews ask to be forgiven by God and their peers, we stand as a congregation and recite a litany of sins for which we wish to be forgiven. Many of them involve acts of speech.

> *For the sin we have sinned against You through foul speech.*
> *For the sin we have sinned against You by fraud and falsehood.*
> *For the sin we have sinned against You by idle chatter.*
> *For the sin we have sinned against You by false oaths.*
> *For the sin we have sinned against You through slander.*
> *For the sin we have sinned against You through gossip.*
> *For the sin we have sinned against You by judging others.*[15]

When I feel compelled to speak, I have several choices. I can say something positive; I can say something negative; I can choose not to speak when in fact I should; I can choose to keep silent for a time and listen.

I could choose one of the above, and unintentionally that choice could be a mistake. There are a hundred variations of good and a hundred of bad, and all the while the world I see is being formed and those who see me are discovering who I am. It's a tricky business, this power of words. We carry a sword and a flower, a curse and a blessing. And so much of the time we are careless and even unaware, like a teenager behind the driver's wheel with a beer in his hand.

We must be aware of what we say and what we should but don't say, and when we choose to keep silent. I can allow words of poetry to flow from my lips or let curses hiss through my teeth. Perhaps that is what is meant by the phrase *I am my prayer to You*. My life itself becomes a prayer to all that is holy when the quality of my speech brings light and love to the world instead of despair.

It's really quite frightening when you think about what's at stake.

The land beneath my feet is soft and uneven, and so I walk with a staff for comfort and guidance. I walk trying to notice blessing and beauty, to build a world of goodness and peace. Sometimes I walk with a companion, and we speak of our dreams and fears. Sometimes we are gentle and sometimes we are not. And so the staff that guides me has two ends, always in opposition; speech and silence are my guides. It takes practice, finesse, and awareness to know when to speak and when to keep silent.

When my own words fail me, when they seem to be lowly or are simply absent, I pull out a phrase, a poem, or a prayer that others have written. It is good to memorize great lines, which can elevate your thoughts and the quality of your speech. It is proper not to stand alone when there is so much to say in a world of senseless chatter. Stand with the great poets of the centuries; draw on their words to express what needs to be said.

My God, stop my tongue from speaking evil, and my lips from speaking deceit.[16] May the words of my mouth and the meditations of my heart be acceptable to You, my God, my Rock and my Redeemer.[17]

Janet Fitch writes in *White Oleander*, "Always learn poems by heart…they become the marrow in your bones. Like fluoride in the water, they'll make your soul impervious to the world's decay."[18]

PERSPECTIVE:
THE LANGUAGE OF
THOUGHT

I Declare...

I declare independence
From every thought gone wild,
From every laughter
  armed with ridicule.
I declare independence
  from fear,
From hatred,
From every idea gone astray,
From every setting sun.
I declare independence
  from fallen tears,
From unsettling doubt.

No child should feel
The miserable hand of loss.

I declare independence
  from all I seek
And shall never have.
I declare that no man or
women
Will ever dictate my life's
course.

With every setting sun,
And every rising moon,
I declare my soul's peace.

I declare independence
  from menace,
From deliberate pain.

I declare independence for
Every fallen tree,
For every wounded animal,
I declare independence
From every wasted breath,
From prejudice and pride,
From unwanted nightmares.

The stars have yet to shine
And every declaration
  of independence
Has yet to be heard,
And yet I declare my
  independence
With an ever growing mind.
—TALIA KEDAR

CHOICE AS A SPIRITUAL LAW

I am mystified by the paradox of the human spirit. It is both fragile and resilient. It is easily bruised and yet protected from permanent damage. It can spend a lifetime as a darkened shadow, and it can survive like an ember among dead coals. What is the difference between the soul that has risen from the ashes and the one that has disintegrated into gray powder? The paradox of the human spirit is mystifying. Why do some people survive the utter hell of their circumstances while others crumble?

It seems that we make a choice at some point in our lives. There are those who choose to develop and nurture a strong spiritual center. At first this decision is neither conscious nor noble. It simply feels like survival. Somewhere deep inside a voice shouts at the darkness, "No! Not me! You will not get me." And there are others who run, hide, and submerge, deadening themselves at the center. They choose safety in the form of retreat, creating a shell so effective that it indeed deadens the pain but also deadens the joy of a spiritual life.

Retreat is not to be criticized. It is done in the name of survival. Nor is it a tactic that must be permanent. We always stand in the moment of choice. At any time we can decide to choose differently, and therefore live differently. At any moment that voice from within can announce in defiance, "No! Not me! You will not get me."

I was about to learn about the mystical power of the spirit that chooses blessing as I rushed into Starbuck's one early Monday morning to meet a friend. I was late, and it took me a few minutes to settle in and relax. We sat, sipped, exchanged pleasant conversation about work, husbands, children.

Suddenly Jane said to me, "What do you know about the Sabbath song 'Shalom Aleichem'?" I looked at my friend and smiled. This is what I like most about her, her thirst for Torah, her intellectual rigor, her need to know more. I knew what she was really asking. Jane wanted to find a rabbinic commentary, perhaps a Talmudic passage or a midrash, explaining that simple song we sing at the beginning of our Sabbath meal:

Welcome, ministering angels, messengers of the Most High, the Supreme Ruler of All, the Holy and Blessed One.

Enter in peace, you angels of peace, messengers of the Most High, the Supreme Ruler of all, the Holy and Blessed One.

May you go in peace, O angels of peace, messengers of the Most High, the Supreme Ruler of all, the Holy and Blessed One.

A simple, sweet song, I thought. A song that welcomes the angels to our Shabbat meal, no more, no less.

"Why do you ask?"

I watched Jane take a long sip of her coffee. Then she told me the story she heard from a woman at a national leadership convention.

Let me tell you how we survived the Holocaust.

The Allies were liberating the camps, and there was mass confusion. The Nazis tried to shoot everyone they could. My brother and I survived Auschwitz by hiding deep in the latrines. The filth and stench were unbearable, but so was our fear of being killed, so we went in so far, no Nazi would dare enter. To keep our sanity, we decided to sing songs. There we stood, up to our waists in filth, and we turned to one another, held hands, and sang the songs we used to sing around the Sabbath table.

Then a strange thing happened. It was so odd. The Nazis didn't seem to hear us, but the children did. As we sang "Shalom Aleichem," other children who were also running for their lives heard our voices and came into the latrine and sang with us. There we stayed for a long while, singing.

This is how we survived Auschwitz.

Jane repeated her question: "What do you know about 'Shalom Aleichem'?"

Intrigued and challenged, I went back to my office and began pulling books off my library shelf. Rather quickly my search took me to a familiar Talmudic passage:

As you leave the synagogue Friday night you are accompanied by a good angel and a bad angel. As you enter your home, if you find the candles lit for the Sabbath and the home pre-pared, then the good angel says "May all your Sabbaths be like this." And the bad angel, despite his nature, must say amen. But if you enter your home and do not find the candles lit and the table prepared for the Sabbath, then the bad angel says, "May all your Sabbaths be like this." And the good angel, despite her nature, must say amen.[1]

In the filth and stench of an Auschwitz latrine, in the midst of the ultimate evil of the universe, those children held hands and chose the blessing of the Sabbath. With the sweetness of their voic-es raised in song, they evoked the good angels of peace, calling to the children to come and take refuge. Into the filth came beauty, into death and evil came life and blessing. Despite their nature, the evil forces were forced to say amen to the lives of these children.

We cannot control what happens to us. That is clear. The chil-dren of Buchenwald did not choose to die. The mothers of Treblinka did not choose to leave their children. The fathers of

Dachau did not choose to starve to death. There was little choice in the death camps but for one crucial exception: The victims had control over their spirit. They could choose how to react to their horrid circumstances.

This choice is called spiritual resistance. The Nazis could terrorize, murder, and destroy, but ultimately they could not control the spirit that chose to resist.

Marion Woodman was stricken with cancer as she began to keep her journal. Her prognosis was grim, but her determination and resolve were great. She wrote, "What I learned is the difference between fate and destiny. We are all fated to die. Destiny is recognizing the radiance of the soul that even when faced with human impossibility, loves all of life. Fate is the death we owe to nature. Destiny is the life we owe to soul."[2]

What is my destiny? What life must live through me, and how do I brace myself against the twists and turns so that it can? The paradox of the human spirit is mystifying. Why do some people survive the utter hell of their circumstances while others crumble? A decision is made to choose to be strengthened by life rather than defeated. Without hope, there are those who curl up on the side of the spiritual road.

ENVISION

How do we draw the diagram of the spiritual universe? I want to map its boundaries, its mountain peaks and canyons. I want to understand what characterizes the rules and roads of the spiritual pathways. Where are my guides, what are they trying to say? The rabbis of the Talmudic period tell us that the world stands on three things, or ten behaviors, or three values, or on the absolute one endeavor that can summarize a life with all its richness. In discussion after discussion the rabbis try to find the right combination, which will capture the essence, the spirit of life's purpose and meaning.

   In one particular teaching, the rabbis say that when you die (you should live one hundred and twenty years) and you are perched on the edge of eternity, you will be asked six questions before you are allowed to enter. What an intriguing thought. Six questions. What would they be, what should they be, have I anticipated them, have I lived their answer? Six questions that reflect a life of spiritual decency:

1. Were you honest in business?
2. Did you apportion fixed times for study?
3. Did you engage in procreation? (Did you raise up disciples?)
4. Did you envision salvation?
5. Did you delve into matters of wisdom?
6. Have you understood one thing from another?[3]

All the questions are worthy of great consideration, but it is the fourth that teaches the spiritual law of perception. *Tzapita l'yeshua?* the rabbis ask. Did you envision salvation? The word *tzapita* comes from the Hebrew root that means "to envision," "to hope," and "to expect" all in one. There is a great connection between hope and vision. What I see when I look beyond the horizon depends on my ability to hold hope in my heart.

To enter eternity, it seems, I must see the world through a certain perspective, envisioning a time when all will be just and fine. When the Spirit of the Universe will reconcile all that makes me inconsolable. Where hope is as natural and obvious as the beating of my heart. Where I can foresee a future in which the dreams of the innocent prevail and the hopes of the courageous rule the earth. How do I envision salvation, even though I do not know exactly what it means to live there? So much depends on my perspective.

In the summer, Israel is hot and dusty. The air is thick and heavy, and there is dust far and near. It blurs the horizon and stings my nostrils as I try to breathe through the heat. Because of the dust, I hate to drive with the windows open. The hot wind causes my eyes to sting and gives my hair a gritty feel. Yet there we were, driving sixty miles an hour on a one-lane highway, high noon with windows open, radio blasting and dust attacking, when I saw a sight that stunned me. It was a field of sunflowers.

I had never seen sunflowers before. I had believed the artist and the cartoonist and my imagination; I envisioned them as beautiful and exotic flowers that looked like their name, happy bursts of sun. But they're not that at all. They are large, clumsy, and rather ugly. Sunflowers grow in a brown and dusty field. Their stems are long, brownish green, and weedlike. There is very little flower, only scarce and scraggly yellow petals surrounding a disproportionately large center of black seeds that stare out at the world like the eye of a frightened creature, which will never shut. This eye is large and heavy and causes the flower to droop pathetically.

Then I understood. A sunflower is called a sunflower not because it looks like the sun, but because it looks *for* the sun.

This clumsy flower is in perpetual motion; it turns, following the sun as it moves across the sky. It seeks the light most aggressively so that it may grow and feed the seeds, which are its core. Therein lies the poetry that captures the heart of the artist: It is not the way this awkward flower looks, but rather the way it behaves. The sunflower must find the sun and nurture its seeds, and it bids us to do the same. It calls us to understand that hope is the perpetual tracking of the light that will feed our core and nourish the seeds of our dreams.

To survive and triumph, to forgive, we must learn to hope eternally. We hope for meaning and purpose to ultimately be revealed. We hope that goodness is truly the foundation of the considered life. We hope that as we proceed, we do so with beauty and grace by our side. We hope that all will be OK and that like the sunflower, our hearts will ultimately turn toward the warmth and nourishment they need to grow. As the sun is to the sunflower, hope is to the human spirit, for without hope, there is despair and darkness.

Can you envision salvation?

Hope is a choice. Hope is not a prenatal disposition or a fate granted or denied by the gods of some imagined world. Hope is a choice we can make at any given moment. One way to make that choice is to ask the question: Is this thought, person, or situation life-affirming or life-draining? If it is life-draining, choose not to engage it, not to give it credence or power. Do not add to your despair. If it is life-affirming, embrace it, and in doing so, you will have chosen to live with the thoughts, people, and situations that will support hope.

In my office sits a plaque created by Mary Engelbreit. It pictures a child with a stick over her shoulder; tied to the stick is a handkerchief containing all her belongings. She faces a crossroads in the woods, and on each path is a wooden signpost. To the right it says "Your Life" and to the left it says, "No Longer an Option."

To envision salvation is to take the path toward the life we dream of living.

MEMORY: LIFE RETOLD OR UNLEARNED

I was on a plane from New York going home, tired from an intense four days of meetings. My eyes burned as I sipped red airplane wine from a clear plastic glass. I was flipping through a magazine and came across the words "Ogunquit, Maine." Smiling, I put the magazine on my lap, closed my eyes, and returned to a memory I'd forgotten I had.

It begins as we all piled into my cousin Amy's car and drove from Boston to Ogunquit, Maine, to go to the beach. I had never done anything like that before. I was visiting Amy during spring break, and my older cousin seemed so free, unencumbered by parental rules, so fun and adventurous. This was definitely going to be fun. But why was the memory so strong? Something happened that Sunday afternoon that I still can't put into words.

Maybe it was the sand. Thirty years later, and I still know the feeling of Ogunquit sand on the palm of my hand, like cradling a thousand minute pieces of fine white silk. Maybe it was the water. Oh, my God, it was so cold: fifteen seconds, and my feet lost all feeling. But the ocean looked so inviting and blue, not like the green Maryland shore, but like the color of heaven itself. But probably it was Carl. (Or was his name Bill?) At seventeen, an important three years older than I, he was handsome, with long blond hair and blue eyes. He was slender but not too slender, and, most importantly, slightly attentive (though not too attentive) to Amy's little cousin from Maryland.

That's it. That's the memory. I don't remember if we stayed the night at Ogunquit beach or drove back that same day. I don't remember what we ate, or if we laughed, or if we simply lay on towels and sunbathed. All I remember from that summer day is the convergence of beauty: of sand, ocean, and the way the boy smiled at me.

Memory is perhaps one of the most powerful elements in the formation of a person—a certain kind of memory, in which not facts but, rather, intangibles such as sensations, impressions, and scraps of images are the primary resources that shape the way we see the world.

Memory: the convergence of unrelated fragments. The bringing together of pieces of the world in such a way that they tell a story. The linking of thoughts and pictures until they make sense. Memory is the narrative we tell the world and ourselves and that forms the present reality.

The Jewish New Year has many names, among them the Day of Remembrance and the Day of Judgment. The Day of Remembrance asks us to turn around and look into the past for its lessons, its mistakes, its greatness. The Day of Judgment asks us to look ahead, realizing that all our deeds have ramifications and consequences.

Two names for this holy day, which commemorates the creation of the world. To recreate our lives in the New Year, it seems that we are to use the materials of the past to form a vision for the future. This takes great care. Memory can serve as a crutch if we believe that we are somehow crippled, or memory can serve as a foundation for growth; it can make the difference between living in the past and building on the past.

It seems that history is intertwined with destiny; we simply cannot anticipate what lies ahead without remembering what came before. We climb a ladder toward redemption, each rung in the past and yet advancing us to greater heights. We are born to be great storytellers of fantastic tales. All those moments weaving their way through our lives have become the raw material for the plot, the senses, and the images that create our conclusions about what is true and what is not, what is good and what is not, what is likely to happen and what is not.

As we retell the story of our lives, one question is most helpful. What have we learned? Every moment, event, person is an opportunity for learning and is ultimately the foundation for growth. In fact, that may be the difference between someone who lives in the present and one who is frozen in the past. Have you learned the lesson of the moment? Until you do, you will not move on.

I know a seventy-year-old woman who repeatedly tells the story of being the most beloved by her mother of all the siblings. I must have heard this story a hundred times or more. Now I wonder if she learned from that loving experience. Did she ever learn in the depth of her soul that she is beloved because she is worthy of love, or does she still need her mother to whisper, in her memory, tender words?

Memory is not only a personal possession. It is also shared as a common link in community. For a brief time during my days as a seminary student, I served a congregation in Selma, Alabama. In Selma, they often refer to the War between the States. When I asked, "Do you mean the Civil War?" they smiled at my provincial northeast astonishment and patiently replied that that was indeed the war they were referring to. When I returned to school I mentioned the conversation to a classmate who was from Sumter, South Carolina. He too smiled at me and then said, "They were just being polite. When I was in school they taught us about the 'War of Northern Aggression.'"

The Civil War, the War between the States, the War of Northern Aggression all speak to the same event, but a different reality. This was so odd, so dramatic in my mind, that it stayed with me as a gnawing question. How do the words we use change the way we experience the memory of a past event in the present?

Years later I tried an experiment. While teaching high school students about the Holocaust, I wrote "World War II" on the blackboard and asked them to give me their associations. Quickly the board filled with images of GI Joe, American soldiers, beautiful blonde German spies, U-boats, submarines, John Wayne. Then I wrote the word "Holocaust," and the board filled with items like death camps, SS officers, extermination of the Jews, Nazis. I asked my students, "Do you know, I mean really know, that the Holocaust happened during World War II?" Clearly on some level they did not. The same historical event, described in different words, creates a different understanding

And so I learned that the way we remember an event influences the way we experience the present. The way we tell the story, the words we use to relate the details of the story, the images and emotions we choose to express the truth of the story, all shape the lasting impact that story has on our lives.

It's not only what we remember, but also what we choose to ignore that can inform our spiritual lives and create for us a healthy balance. So many voices have told us what we can do and what we can't. They have defined for us failure, unlived potential, and success. Part of becoming whole is learning when not to listen to the lessons.

It was in third grade, as a student of Mrs. Bradshaw, that I was taught that I was simply and sadly average. Mrs. Bradshaw never really smiled. She was tall and thin with dark hair pulled tightly behind her neck. I do not remember her eyes; I have only a vague impression of her face as sort of pale and angry. On every report card, she gave me two B's and the rest C's. No matter what I did or didn't do, I got two B's and the rest C's. The rhythm of that phrase still feels like a chant beating mediocrity into my brain, like the drums of a threatening tribe.

Mrs. Bradshaw's class is where I learned that I would never be good at math, that I wasn't living up to my potential, and that the strong really do have power over the weak. When it came time to learn to write in cursive, we were called to the board in threes to copy Mrs. Bradshaw's perfect handwriting, which spelled out *cat, hat, bat....* When I approached the board I would take the chalk in my left hand, and Mrs. Bradshaw would announce loud enough for everyone to hear, "I can't teach you, you're left-handed."

It was in third grade, as a student of Mrs. Bradshaw, that I learned the power and wonder of my imagination. Not being able to learn, having been declared unteachable and too lazy for excellence, I began to dream and imagine and fantasize. I pretended to be Cinderella, waiting to be discovered as the beautiful princess I was sure I was. I played with my trolls secretly under my desk, pretending to be the mayor of a village of trolls. They were small dolls with lovely long hair, potbellies, and ugly-cute faces, and I loved them. I wrote my first short story, entitled "The Orange That Spoke to Me," about an orange with special powers granting me three wishes. It had a plot, an illustrated cover, and, of course, a wonderful ending.

Then it happened.

As usual, Mrs. Bradshaw called me up to the board as part of the next group to practice cursive handwriting, and as she passed by me she announced, as she had in the past, that I could not be taught because I was left-handed. I went back to my place and looked down at the paper on my desk. It was a newsprint color with blue lines that were generously spaced apart. My lead pencil was smooth and thick so little hands could easily grasp it.

I began to draw my letters, and as I drew a line, I was struck by the magic of writing. "What a miracle," I remember thinking. With slow, deliberate strokes, a line became a letter. A letter turned into a word. A word stretched into a sentence. Each sentence spun a thought. Every thought created a world. I was struck with awe and reverence at the power I possessed. Here I was, an average and rather mediocre student, and yet I had extraordinary powers to create.

I finished third grade with two B's and the rest C's. But I went into the summer before fourth grade as a writer of words and thoughts.

Our lives are a remarkable string of countless tales that beg to be retold. Our spiritual and emotional lives today are composed of these tales. There was the time we were loved, the time we were ignored, the time the teacher implied that we were stupid, the time our best friend betrayed us, the time when we first loved deeply and completely, the time we were bored, the time when we were hopeful that things would work out, the time when nobody listened, the time when we were in the center of the world.

When you think of these moments, what picture do you paint? When you speak these memories, what words do you use? Do you emphasize the blessing or the curse? When you tell the story, stay away from anger and resentment; try to focus the telling on the life lessons learned by overcoming an obstacle. When you tell the story, do not minimize the success; explain how the experience propelled you to your current place. At first this may be difficult, particularly if you have told an event a certain way for years.

Healing is in the retelling. Wholeness is found as we reframe the story. It makes a difference how we choose to remember.

Our life is lived in all directions at once; past, present and future are at times indistinguishable in the way they create our reality. We use the past to judge the future. In this way our perception of the moment is formed. What I have been reaches into the dream of what I can be. I must learn to use the past as a foundation instead of a crutch, as a series of blessings not curses, as lessons that I have embraced, and then reach even beyond what I believe is possible.

I sometimes think that my life depends on my ability to go to the outer limits of what I believe to be true. That I somehow must play with my perceptions of the past in order to go past any limitations I have learned along the way. That my reach for greatness, beauty, and peace depends upon what I believe is likely—which depends upon what I have seen as possible. This is my prayer:

God, cleanse my memory of shadows and pain,
Help me see that I have been truly blessed
So that I may receive Your blessing.
Whisper to my soul melodies of long-ago love.
With songs of love as my past,
Visions of hope will be my destiny.

REFLECTION, THEN REACTION

We were in a hurry to leave the house, fearing that we would be late to get somewhere. My mother stepped outside the front door, straightened her shoulders, buttoned the top of her coat tight around her neck, took out her car gloves, and pronounced, "It's raw out today." For years I would experience this little ritual, and yet I wasn't quite sure what temperature "raw" was. Sometimes it seemed unbearably cold and dry, like an angry day in late January. Other times it was damp and cloudy with a drizzle that heralded the coming of spring. Then there was the time she said it was raw on a perfectly fine fall day whose only flaw was a slight chill in the breeze. I was confused by the rawness my mother felt, and yet as a child I learned to live with the ambiguity. It was one of those things that children simply do not understand.

Indeed.

Yesterday I was at the kosher market buying a dinner of cold cuts, potato salad, cole slaw, and fresh rolls to go along with dried fruit for our Tu B'Shevat celebration. It was a gray day in February, but we were in a warming trend. In Israel, Tu B'Shevat, the New Year of the Trees, is celebrated as the beginning of spring. Almond trees, which can be found in abundance on the side of the road and in open fields, are all abloom with their pastel pink buds. The children sing songs to these delightful trees, happy at the change of seasons. They go out to the hills and plant saplings as part of a national reforestation plan in Israel. It's a bit of a disconnect to celebrate this holiday here in America, but we do the best we can, eating dried fruit, telling stories, describing the sites of the Land of Israel. We celebrate the great miracle of trees by sending money to plant a tree in Israel in the name of someone we love.

The butcher wrapped the last of my sliced turkey and handed me the credit card slip to sign. Making polite conversation, he asked me, "Is it nice outside?"

"It's raw," I said with great authority. I pulled my coat around me and put on my gloves for emphasis. I didn't think anything of it until I got home. I went into the house and with great effort put away the groceries. I was so tired. Here it was in the middle of the day, and I could barely move. I made a cup of hot tea and sank onto my couch to rest, just for a minute, before the kids got home. I was feeling the kind of exhaustion that makes every cell of your being ache with heaviness. Sipping my tea, I heard a bird sing. I looked outside and saw the sun shining, the snow melting, and the birds flying from tree to tree.

Then I understood. It wasn't raw outside. It was raw inside.

Raw is the spiritual scraping of the bone.

My mother was not teaching me the finer points of climate and weather. She was giving me a vocabulary to describe the internal waxing and waning of a spiritual life. Raw described the moonless night of the soul. "It's raw outside" means "It's ever so painful inside," a kind of rawness, tender to the core, vulnerable to the world, sensitive to the touch. And now that I recall, those days when my mother said it was "raw" were days when we children were careful not to be overly annoying, imposing, or demanding. She simply wasn't up to it.

So here I sit, on my couch, on a perfectly good day, children are healthy, husband is fine, work is wonderful, the day outside is temperate and yet I feel...well, rather raw.

So much of what we experience is a reflection of our internal lives. We have a natural filter, a bias that processes what goes in and what comes out so that no thought or reaction is pure or independent of our personal history, our mood, our assumptions about what is true and right, or even our soul's journey. Perspective is a matter of seeing things a certain way and reacting to them. But we can change the way we see things, and we can change the way we react.

If any given moment is to be consistent with reality, rational thought, and spiritual balance, we must be aware of our reaction to that moment as it is reflected by our inner world. A beautiful day becomes raw because we believe it to be so; we react to the world from the inside out.

Our inner world, the world of the soul and thought and the world of emotion and spirit, all live in a swirl of dust and glitter, of light and shadow. In this swirl, love and fear dance as partners in paradox. Deep in the core of our being, we know we have been given a gift of divine love and are loved unconditionally, that the universe is abundant in possibility and love, and that we are worthy of those gifts.

And yet, at the same time, we fear that we will not be loved or accepted, that there is not enough in the universe to provide for us unconditionally, that we have been born into some cruel game of tit-for-tat. We fear we are not worthy of others' love and so we withhold our own, lest we run out. We live an internal paradox: we believe that we are loved and despised, that we are entitled and denied, that we are essentially good. Well, sort of.

The way we act and react to the complexities of our lives directly correlates to that internal swirl of shadow and glitter, of love and fear. The paradox of love and fear is to be recognized and handled, as a man handles a woman on the dance floor, with both strong intent and graceful acquiescence to the push and pull of movement and partnership. I do not know anyone completely free of fear or for whom love is completely absent. Both are a part of being, just as light is both particle and wave.

Much of our response to life stems from love or fear. Negative emotions such as anger, guilt, anxiety, and helplessness are generated by fear, by that aspect of ourselves that is sure we will not be loved and supported by God, by the world, by the individuals in our lives. So much of the spiritual principle of perspective depends on how we interact and react to fear-based emotions.

The native women of Vancouver Island tell the story of the great and horrifying Sisiutl, who is a snakelike creature who lives in the water:

> Sisiutl sees from the front and the back. Sisiutl the soul searcher. He seeks those who cannot control their fear, who do not have a Truth.
>
> When you see Sisiutl the terrifying, though you be frightened, stand firm; there is no shame in being frightened, only a fool would not be afraid of Sisiutl the horror. Stand firm, and if you know protective words say them. First one head, then the other, will rise from the water. Closer. Closer. Coming for your face, the ugly heads, closer, and the stench from the devouring mouths, and the cold, and the terror. Stand firm. Before the twin mouths of Sisiutl can fasten on your face and steal your soul, each head must turn toward you. When this happens, Sisiutl will see his own face.
>
> Who sees the other half of Self, sees Truth.
>
> Sisiutl spends eternity in search of Truth. In search of those who know Truth. When he sees his own face, his own other face, when he looks into his own eyes, he has found Truth.
>
> He will bless you with magic, he will go, and your Truth will be yours forever. Though at times it may be tested, even weakened, the magic of Sisiutl, his blessing, is that your Truth will endure.[4]

The Truth of our lives is an eternal abiding love from the Holy One. The Truth is that we are worthy of this love. The Truth is that our private vision of a self that is whole, content, and competent is not a fantasy. The Truth is that there are very few days that are raw, if our perspective allows for beauty and blessing. What banishes the Truth is fear that all that is not really true. We live in that paradox, but "who sees the other half of Self, sees Truth."

Reaction must constantly be tempered with reflection. Reflect on the source of your words, your actions, or your thoughts. Are they based on fear or love? Notice when fear is motivating you. Search for the loving intention of all things. For the universe abounds with goodness and love. May that understanding be the waters from which you draw.

Martin Buber writes, "Man can see his reflection in the water only when he bends close to it, and the heart of man too must lean down to the heart of his fellow; then it will see itself within his heart."[5]

LINGERING

We were having Shabbat dinner with good friends. Our children were busy at play, the teenagers engaged in conversations of great consequence, the adults sipping yet one more glass of Merlot, when my friend Arna said suddenly, "Why don't we go to Paris and hear David sing at Notre Dame?" Our friend David was a member of an adult male choir that performed every few years in different spots around the world. This particular summer it was to be High Mass at Notre Dame. I took a sip of wine and looked at Arna's large brown eyes. I could tell she was serious, sort of. "OK," I said. "Let's go to Paris and hear David sing at Notre Dame."

After considering the pros and cons, discussing who would join us and who would not, and trying to work out the difficult logistics, I purchased a ticket for myself and one for each of my daughters, who would be in Israel at the time and would be meeting me in Paris a couple of days after my arrival. That gave me two days in Paris alone before my daughters arrived, and then another day alone with the girls before Arna and her family joined us.

As news of my trip spread among my friends, I acquired lists of museums, sights to see, guidebook titles. And yet all I really wanted to do was sit in Parisian cafés. I went to gather even more information from my local bookstore and found myself reaching for a book called *The Cafés of Paris*. That's what I'll do, I thought; I'll go to Paris and drink coffee. The more I thought about it, the more I became enchanted with the idea. I politely tucked away the lists of museums and historic sites and secretly read about the cafés. I discovered that it was around a table on a sidewalk in Paris that Jean Paul Sartre and Simone de Beauvoir met, spoke and wrote, and fell in love. I bought a copy of *The Second Sex*, a brand-new notebook with empty pages fresh with hospitality, and a new pen. I was packed for Paris.

The cafés of Paris entered my soul with resounding truth. The sidewalks of Paris are crowded with small round tables and chairs. At first glance there was something odd about this sight, though it was hard to put my finger on exactly what it was. Then as I went to sit at a café, I realized what it was. All the chairs face the street. They are not clustered around the very small tables, but rather seem to stand at attention in a row, facing the sidewalk, the street, and beyond. To sit at a café in Paris is to be in wordless conversation with the world. One drinks slowly, stares intensely, and thinks with silent clarity.

This is what it is like to linger, I thought.

I spent two days alone, sitting, drinking coffee, eating baguettes with butter and jam, breathing in the city and its people. This is what I witnessed from the sidewalk cafés in Paris: For Parisians, coffee is a destination, one to be experienced. I would time after time watch people as they approached the café. A man in a very fashionable dark business suit with briefcase in hand would be walking rather fast. He would approach the café and hesitate. At first I thought he was waiting for someone, but then I realized that he was lingering, contemplating his next move. He would back up a few steps, look into the café, then back at the street. I could almost hear him debate with himself, weighing the pros and cons—drink a cup of coffee or close a million-dollar deal...coffee, million-dollar deal...coffee, million-dollar deal. Slowly he would turn toward the small tables on the sidewalk, take a seat facing the world, take out a cigarette, and order coffee. There he would linger, half an hour or more. Smoking a cigarette, sipping his espresso, watching with dreamy intensity. Then suddenly he would rise, pay the bill, and go off to his important business deal.

I witnessed this scene several times and would become sad as I juxtaposed this experience with how we Americans "do" coffee. We stand in line at the local Starbuck's, order a skinny grande something or other, hold the whipped cream, take it in a paper cup and run off, slightly annoyed that we had to wait in line.

We have lost our patience; we have simply buried it among the infinite tasks that vibrate with false urgency. Banished by the frantic pace, gentle patience eludes us like a beautiful fall day obscured by the walls of an inner office. I remember reading the journals of women who lived on the prairie during the days of homesteading and log cabins. I kept thinking that without a telephone, you'd actually have to walk a long, slow mile just to say hello.

Patience is not to be found in a hurry.

I must linger to find it. I have not learned, nor have I taught, the spiritual principle of lingering. I cannot be present if I do not linger. And when I am not present, I lose the essence of each moment. To have a clear perspective on just about anything, I must wait a long minute. I have to linger, allowing things to settle a bit, allowing the world to wrap gently around my soul. To have any kind of perspective on things, I must take time to breathe, just breathe, lost in speechless thought. I must invite the world to dance, as it deems fit, without my frantic intervention. Surrender to the rhythm of the snow blowing across a Minnesota lake, linger among the people on a busy street, pause in a room of busy chatter, and notice the dance. Sit to drink your coffee. Breathe for just a moment, as many moments as possible, and get lost in the perfection of it all.

Multitasking seems to be a battle cry for a war no one has clearly defined. If it is the answer, and many think it is, what was the question? The truth is that there is a dark side to multitasking. One must banish the single clear presence of the moment. To linger is to pull out of the knotted ball of thread one clear strand of blue and stare in awe. Walker Evans, the great photographer of the Depression, is quoted as saying, "Stare. Staring is the way to educate the eye. Stare, cry, listen, eavesdrop. Die knowing something. We are not here long." Multitasking will put you in the world of accomplishment but not in the world of knowing.

WATCH

The day is gray, and it's raining ice. The ice from heaven is so fine that it doesn't make any noise as it hits the snow; it just piles up in translucent layers like Maryland mica, catching the reflection of the dull light that manages to escape the clouds. Strained light, like the color of mashed peas fed to a baby.

I light two candles to arm myself against a constant sense of impending melancholy. The vanilla fragrance, the playful dance of flame, Pat Metheny coming through my headphones—these are more powerful than any flu vaccination. The wind is picking up outside. I can't see the ice falling but I know it's there, I can't feel the cold though I'm aware of it, I can't see the end of this Chicago winter though I know it will come.

This moment is to be noticed. All of it: what I know and what I assume, what I sense and what I imagine. Just as it is, not judged, not dreaded, and certainly not denied, but noticed. Noticed and then acknowledged. What passes through our souls must be stated lest it flow through us like water seeping through plaster walls— you may see a spot but you do not know its source. Annie Dillard writes, "Seeing of course is very much a matter of verbalization. Unless I call my attention to what passes before my eyes I simply won't see it."[6]

And so I write out loud, as the sun disappears invisibly at 4:30 P.M. by the natural command of the month of February, and I know

73

now, more than ever, that sometimes meaning has to be watched for.

The story is told:

The king of Israel was expected to travel through the village on a certain day. Even though he was blind, Rabbi Sheshet joined the villagers who gathered to see him go by.

Knowing that the rabbi was blind, a cynic said, "People take whole pitchers to the river to fetch water, but of what use is it to take a broken pitcher to the river?" The blind rabbi understood what the cynic really meant: what is the point of a blind man waiting to see the king?

Rabbi Sheshet answered, "Fool. I will show you that not only will I know when the king arrives, but I'll show you that I am able to understand what is happening better than one who has vision."

When the legion of soldiers appeared, the cynic joined the crowd in shouting, "The king is coming."

"No he is not," the blind rabbi said. And as predicted, the legion went by without the king.

A second legion marched down the road toward the center of the village and again the cynic joined the crowd and shouted, "The king is coming."

Again the rabbi said the king was not coming and once again he was right.

A third legion marched by and this time the crowd fell silent. But Rabbi Sheshet exclaimed, "Now the king is coming!"

When he saw the king, the puzzled cynic asked, "How were you able to tell?"

The rabbi answered, "We learn that long ago, Israel waited for God to pass by. When a powerful wind blew through the mountains, even giant rocks were shattered into stones but God was not in the wind. Then after the wind an earthquake came. But God was not in the earthquake. Then there was a great fire but God was not in the fire. After the fire," the rabbi continued, "a still small voice was heard and God was found in that hush. It was the hush of the crowd that told me that the king was coming."

As the procession passed the blind rabbi offered a private blessing for the king, but the cynic understood that Rabbi Sheshet was also blessed.[7]

The king in the parable is God. The rabbis saw great power in metaphors of royalty and imagined that we all live in the shadow of God's great palace. We indeed live much of our lives in the shadows, but they are shadows of thought, of greatness, of unfulfilled dreams, or simply shadows that are dark and blank. But what would it be like to live in the shadow of godliness? A place that is cool and protecting against the harshness of the world, a place where we feel comfort, love. How would it be to live as if God casts a shadow of divine holiness upon every possible moment, as it is written: "Hide me, shelter me in the shadow of your wings, O God"?[8]

Now, there's a place I'd like to live.

The great Rabbi Sheshet teaches us that to watch for the Divine we must see in a special way. To watch is to consider, and to consider is to understand. In Hebrew, the root words "to watch" and "to consider," l'hitbonen, and "to understand," havanah, are from the same root. In fact, the word for divine and intuitive wisdom, binah, is derived from that same root. There is, it seems, a correlation between watching and the discovery of divine wisdom.

I'm watching the sun fall invisibly behind the curtain of clouds and I see no breathtaking sunset or play of color and light. Just shadows. Slowly the view goes from dull, to gray, to dark, to even darker, and I believe, like the rabbis, that this moment is grand because I am watching for Divinity. The world passes us by with drama and subtlety. What is most noisy seems to get our attention most often, and yet in the hush of ice falling on snow we have a chance to learn something new, and through the learning of it, perhaps see the world differently. Greatness is to be watched for. Holiness is to be watched for.

I am perpetually challenged to watch for the heartbeat of the world in order to gain a new perspective, one that will bring me greater balance. I watch with my eyes and strain my soul to see, but it takes practice to see meaning in ice falling on snow. It is contrary to old habits to hear the breathing of the earth and feel the movement of the shadow. Seeing is believing, but what we see is always subject to interpretation because there is little in life that comes into focus with absolute clarity. So we measure what we see and experience against our beliefs, our assumptions, our history, our fears, our dreams. What hits my mind and soul goes through a filter. It is there, in the processing of information, in the interpretation of the still life from my dining room window, that a new perspective can be found.

So I practice all the time. I watch for meaning.

Mimi, my assistant, and I were driving back to the hotel from a meeting late one night in the central Illinois countryside. We were chatting and I was looking out my window when suddenly I saw the Big Dipper, large as half the Midwest sky, dipping into the horizon. "Stop the car!" I yelled to Mimi. Her reflexes landed us on the side of the road in a snowy embankment.

For the moment I didn't care. I had never before seen this constellation so large, with every star in its formation bright as the twinkle in an angel's eye. It lay on its side as if pouring heaven's goodness onto the earth. I was in awe. We sat there with the window open, the cold winter air on our faces, staring at the stars, not speaking.

Silently, Mimi tried to ease us out of the snow, and as our tires spun, we laughed at the prospect of spending the winter on a desolate Illinois road, stargazing by night, dreaming by day. Despite our nervous fantasy, we made it out of the embankment rather quickly, and as we drove away I kept looking over my shoulder at the stars.

Stargazers have always inspired me. They made a life out of watching for meaning. I read their biographies, trying to discover the formula for creative thinking, the secret to good and fruitful watching. How is it, for example, that everyone looks at the same stars but only some, like Copernicus and Galileo, see unique meaning and revelation?

Galileo was watching a universe driven and loved by God, and yet his mind and soul envisioned a different meaning. He did not reject religion; he simply saw its role differently from others. He did not invent science; he simply interpreted the stars in a new way. He looked out his window at night, often poor, almost always ill and in pain, lonely, having only periodic contact with his cloistered illegitimate daughters. He was usually in danger from men who saw the world through old eyes. He looked out that window and discovered worlds, discovered God, discovered genius.

Galileo writes:

> Whatever the course of our lives, we should receive them as the highest gift from the hand of God, in which equally reposed the power to do nothing whatever for us. Indeed, we should accept misfortune not only in thanks, but in infinite gratitude to Providence, which by such means detaches us from an excessive love for Earthly things and elevates our minds to the celestial and divine.[9]

It is the course of my life, if accepted with gratitude, that can elevate my mind to matters "celestial and divine." Everything is to be noticed and acknowledged as an opportunity to learn, discover, uncover. I look out the window—the windows of home, the car, of my mind—and see what I can see. I listen a bit to my mind and soul conversing about the myriad of meanings that are possible. I eavesdrop on their conversation and do not quiet their ponderings; it is amazing what goes unnoticed.

It is in the conversation between the mind and soul in which creativity scratches at the barriers and we are challenged to see things another way.

"Why do people draw stars with five points?" asks my daughter Shiri. It's a couple of weeks after the Big Dipper encounter, and Shiri is home with the flu. She is doing her science homework. I'm writing this chapter. "Don't they know that stars are balls of light?" she says. The title of her sixth-grade science book is *Discover the Wonder.* I hope she will.

It takes patience, practice, and the belief that if you learn how to watch, you will indeed see great things, that you might even see the King passing by.

INTERPRETATION

Imagine yourself in a cave, Plato writes in *The Republic*. Imagine a place where shadows on the wall, illumined by an unknown light, are your only source of knowing. What would you know? Imagine that you are forever on the floor of this cave, unable to move or turn around, transfixed in a world of illusion, where these shadows are the only reality you know. Imagine, Plato suggests, that even if you could turn to see the light, which you cannot, it would surely blind you.

For the shadow is indeed what you know: just as the sun is apparent to us by the play of light and the shadow it casts, by its reflection in water, and by the light of the moon and stars that contrasts so keenly with the night sky, so is your understanding of Truth a mere shadow on the wall of a cave. And paradoxically, to look at the source of light, to cast your eyes upon the sun directly, is to suffer true blindness.

Most of what I seem to know is what I choose to see, mere shadows and reflections of what is real. Therefore, the power I have to interpret the images of experience is among my greatest powers. Interpretation is a spiritual principle. The world is in constant contact, sending me information, messages, and scenarios to understand. Something happens, I take it in, I understand it, and then I react to it based upon my understanding. Perhaps all is merely illusion. Perhaps the way I see things is a choice.

Victor Frankl writes of a woman who knew she would die within a few days. He is curious about her cheerful state even as she faces death. Frankl quotes her as saying, "I am grateful that fate has hit me so hard…in my former life I was spoiled and did not take spiritual accomplishments seriously." She tells of the only two branches of a chestnut tree that she can see from her bed. The blossoms from the two branches keep her company as she talks to them.

Frankl is not sure whether she is delusional or not and with a bit of sarcasm asks her if they answer her. Yes, they do, she responds. They say, "I am here—I am here—I am life, eternal life."[10]

The shadows become real; they are all I know. They offer me moments of hope or threaten me like lurking ghosts. It depends on how I choose to see it. During her freshman year of high school, my daughter Talia signed up for outdoor education. She had lived most of her life in Israel, where hiking in nature is an ethic, a cultural value. So when she saw the course offered she naturally signed up, expecting to get to know a new group of kids. As it turns out, only three others signed up for the course, and they were all boys (a fact I discovered only after their overnight camping trip). The teacher was preparing them to learn rappelling, and to do so they had to leave the flat land of Illinois for the cliffs of Wisconsin.

There they were—ropes, harnesses, helmets—ready to climb the cliff. Talia told me later that she was really afraid but she was not going to let the three boys see her fear, so she volunteered to be the first one up. She got to the top of the cliff and was overwhelmed by the beauty. The next boy climbed toward the top and she reached for his hand, saying, "Look at this view; how can anyone deny the existence of God?"

"What God?" he asked. "Give me your hand and help me up." He reached the top and the two of them argued over the existence of God.

Talia then broke away from the story to look hard into my eyes. I looked into her thoughtful blue eyes, which are the shape of almonds and the shade of dream. Her gaze told me to brace myself for what came next.

"So Mom," she said, "you know how you go down off a cliff with ropes and harnesses?"

"How?" I ask.

"You go down backwards," she says.

I slow my breathing and wait.

"I was so afraid to go down that this time I went last. I felt my heart pounding, and my hands were white as they grasped the ropes too tightly. I knew they were talking to me, trying to coach me down, but all I could hear was a pounding and a sort of blankness. I slowly inched my way to the edge and went over step by baby step. Suddenly I lost my footing, and I was dangling from the side of the cliff."

Listening to her, I thought, "Thank God I wasn't there." Then, looking at my daughter's thoughtful gaze, I realized that she was teaching me a metaphor for life. Doesn't life feel at times feel like a backward descent off a mountain? Dangling on the edge of sanity or well-being, we think, "I hope the ropes will hold me, I believe the ropes will hold me, I have faith the ropes will hold me."

Talia continued, "There I was hanging, sure I was going to die. Or maybe I was so scared I didn't even think that. I'm sure my teacher was trying to guide me, but I didn't hear anything but the pounding of my heart in my ears. Suddenly, out of the corner of my eye, I saw a shadow of a large bird. It was an eagle or something. It flew so close to me that I thought I felt the wind from its wing.

"And then the strangest thing happened. It was as if this great bird flew by and took all my fear with it. I sat on my harness, no longer scared, and looked around me at the view. I thought to myself, 'I can see 360 degrees of God's creation from here.' I no longer tried to find my footing but rather lingered a while enjoying the great spirit of the moment. Finally I made my descent down the cliff to my friends and teachers."

There was only one difference between the moment in which Talia was hanging from the side of the cliff fearing she was going to die and the moment she was in such awe at God's creation that she didn't rush to safety. The difference was her perspective; it was how she chose to see her circumstance.

I sit cross-legged on the floor of the cave. The shadows have become real, and they are all I know. They offer me moments of hope or threaten me like lurking ghosts. It depends on how I choose to see it. I choose to be elevated by blessing and not to be defeated by curse. Like the ancient ones of the Bible, I ask to be carried by the wings of eagles to redemption. Like the woman who lay dying on her bed, I choose to see the chestnut tree as a message of life eternal.

CHANGE FOR THE SAKE OF TRANSFORMATION

I wonder what it feels like when a snake sheds its skin. Does it hurt, like ripping a bandage from your skin? Does it feel light and clean, like the first haircut of the summer? Is there a sense of sadness and loss, or does the snake feel oddly free of old and familiar constraints?

What does it feel like when that snake forms a new skin? Does it prickle and sting? Does it itch like the healing of a wound? Is there a sense of awe at the newness of it all, or fear that what is new will not be as comfortable as what is old?

What does it feel like during those moments in between? Is that ever-so-thin layer between death and rebirth raw, tender, or numb?

These are, I believe, the sensations experienced during a shift of consciousness. It is not a simple thing to shed the beliefs, assumptions, and perceptions that we hold as tightly as skin to the soul. Yet we must shed them if we are to change in a fundamental way. It is not simple, because our very identity is based on those assumptions. It is not simple, because our beliefs have served us for a lifetime. It is not simple, because to shed a skin, to rip away our self-image, our sense of truth, is terrifying. It is not simple, because we are invested in the way things are. It simply is not simple. We feel like a snake who first sheds its skin, then is skinless, then forms a new one.

Ralph Waldo Emerson writes in his essay *Self-Reliance*, "A foolish consistency is the hobgoblin of little minds.... With consistency a great soul has simply nothing to do. He may as well concern him-self with his shadow on the wall. Speak what you think now in hard words and to-morrow speak what to-morrow thinks in hard words again, though it contradict every thing you said to-day."[11]

Consistency, complacency, and compliance with old ideas nulli-fy any sense that change is essential. They lull us into a sense of stagnation, and we then believe that if it has always been this way, it will always be this way.

The spiritual path is never straight. Rather, we travel it like the sailor who, in order to move forward, tacks from one point to another. At times we find ourselves zigzagging, thinking that we must always move forward, precisely and concisely. We fail to rec-ognize that the crooked path is indeed a path, though it could make you dizzy. As we travel this path we perpetually change our vantage point. We see things, including ourselves, from a different angle, for the points of reference are forever shifting. Moving along on our spiritual journey, we are asked to examine all that is previously thought to be true.

We cannot change without experiencing change. We cannot grow without growing. We cannot rise to the next level of under-standing without leaving the level that has been our perch for so long. So why do we resist change all the time when it is a basic fact of life?

To change we must simply live, but to experience transforma-tion we must undergo a sort of collapse, or a stripping of what we thought to be true.

Lisa, Carol, and I were sitting on the living room floor around a smoky glass table perched on a black marble slab that offended my aesthetic sensibilities but was large enough for an array of lit can-dles, partially empty notebooks waiting to be filled, pens, pretzels, and, of course, Chardonnay. It was summer, warm, and the glow of the candlelight caressed us like a lullaby. We spoke softly, random-ly, and in turn. Our thoughts created a circle of logic, attaching thoughts to thoughts until scraps of unrelated material became a quilt of great variety. All night we had been pondering why and where. Why had our lives unfolded the way they had, and where were we to venture next? But mostly, we were there to offer courage to one another, courage to bear the lessons of the past and courage to step into the lessons of the future, courage to see change as an opportunity rather than a threat.

"When I was a child, I had a recurring dream," I began. I had never told the dream before to anyone, for two seemingly opposite reasons. The dream seemed at once inconsequential and extraordinarily private.

"What was your dream about?" they asked in unison.

"Well, I'm not sure what it was about. It was quite simple, actually. I dreamt over and over that I was a squirrel, gray, soft, and very busy. All I did was run back and forth gathering acorns and bringing them to a hollow of a tree."

"That's it?"

"That's it," I said. "That's the whole dream. Strange, isn't it? I loved this dream. It made me feel safe. I used to fall asleep asking the maker of dreams to send it to me that night."

We went on to another subject and talked late into the night. Lisa went home, and Carol was spending the night. Carol and I were getting ready for bed and were about to turn out the light when the phone rang. It was Lisa. Excitedly she whispered, so as not to wake her sleeping family, "I looked up squirrels in a book I have on Native American lore, which interprets the symbolic meaning of animals. The squirrel gathering acorns and hiding them in the hollow of a tree represents a person who is storing her wisdom for a long spiritual winter." I was stunned. In a flash of Native American wisdom, I understood a persistent message of my childhood. I understood that as I lay asleep, I was reassuring myself that all would be OK.

Remembering what it felt like to be a little girl, I crawled into bed relishing the heavy protection of my covers despite the warm night. In the dark floating moments before the cave of deep sleep,

I reviewed my early years, like a director watching the unedited version of his film. Storing my wisdom for a long winter was a fine metaphor. Indeed, there had been years of winter-like existence, when I was not recognized for who I was, or perhaps had not recognized myself for who I was becoming. There had been years of spiritual and psychological isolation, self-imposed or otherwise.

Storing my wisdom…was this dream a message from my spirit telling me not to despair, that though the years ahead would be difficult, my essential self—the truth of who I am—was stored for safekeeping?

That night, for the first time since I was a child, the squirrel returned to my dreams. I dreamt that I was in my house, which was large and familiar. I stepped outside and saw a squirrel going in and out of the house at the point where the roof intersects two walls to form a three-pointed corner.

As I watched the squirrel, suddenly the house began to crumble. I thought, "I liked this house. How will I find a place that I like as well?" Then I stood there, on the edge of my lawn, and watched the total collapse of my home. As is so often the case, at night the dream was a curiosity, in the morning it was a revelation. According to some dream theories, the house represents the self. Often when you are experiencing a change, you will dream of discovering a room in a house that until that moment you didn't know existed.

But my dream was different. It was a complete collapse of self, which was caused by the squirrel that symbolized for me innate divine wisdom. My stored wisdom was calling me to a new home. Though in the dream I remember that I liked the house and was sad to see it go, it was because I was invested in the person I had become. But I was at a crossroads in my life. I knew that to progress, to be more of who I could be, I was to abandon old thoughts and beliefs. I was to undergo a collapse of the system of thought that had served me for so long but was beginning to confine me, so that I could discover the more authentic part of who I was—indeed, who I was meant to be.

In his book *The Soul's Code*, James Hillman explains what he calls "the acorn theory." The acorn, though small, contains within its shell all the information needed to become a full-grown oak tree. So it is with people. It is a mistake, he claims, to see our lives simply as the "interplay of genetics and environment." We are more than "a plot written by my genetic code, ancestral heredity, traumatic occasions, parental unconscious, societal accident." Our lives are about character, calling, beauty, mystery. Like the acorn, "each person bears a uniqueness that asks to be lived, and is already present before it can be lived."[12]

And is already present before it can be lived.

The rabbis say that the infant is born knowing everything there is to know. But at the moment of birth, Elijah the Prophet comes to visit and gently touches the space above the newborn's mouth with his finger, leaving a small indentation as a sign that he was there. Having been touched by the mysterious prophet, the baby forgets and then spends the rest of her life trying to remember what she once knew.

~

The God of Wisdom beckons to our souls in the night, in the light, through encounters, and through long silences. The God of Wisdom reminds us who we are, reminds us of our uniqueness, of our calling, of the true meaning and purpose of our lives. The God of Wisdom calls to us through our dreams and visions. It is so easy to be distracted from who we really are. Looking back, I could focus on the cruelty of winter, but instead I focus on the genius of the journey. The difficult years of my youth could easily be relegated to the category of unrealized scenarios and disappointments. But when I remember those early years with curiosity and awe, feeling the emotion of the moment without judgment, I am open to discovering clues to the brilliance of the acorn.

I have been called to shed a skin many times—to change a perspective, an internal barrier that may once have protected me but now serves as a block to growth. I have been called to peel away a persona that simply does not fit the evolving truth of who I am. I have been called not once or even twice, but many times to reconsider what I believe to be true, to strip away assumptions, to form a new skin, born of the raw materials of the old one, but somehow different. I have been called to get out of my way and allow newness and grandeur to emerge. All this and more is the nature of change that becomes transformative. It is the difference between what changes as a matter of course, like the flow in a stream, which knows only perpetual motion, and a moment of redemptive transformation.

I yearn to be different from the center out, to recreate myself somehow, over and over again, from the raw materials of my soul. I ask only to be who I was created to be, each time closer and wiser and better and nearer to the Source of all things.

Creator of the universe, push me, pull me, strip me of what is no longer of service. And as You do, use me, as I unfold like a miracle before my very eyes.

MEANING

INTROSPECTION: LOOKING WITHIN

What is there to say about the inner life?
It is as complex as the watery byways of Venice,
Delicate as the hands of an infant child,
Curious and compact as the wisdom of an acorn.
It is as magnificent as the profile of an African queen.

It eludes comprehension and yet it is ever present,
Enveloping every moment of life.

One lives from the inside out.
A gnarl of emotion, biography, memory, and spirit.
Each blending and bending into the other
Like knotted strands of crocheted comforter.
It is a world I will never truly understand,
And yet the only reality I can ever know.

What lies within yearns for love, support, and courage.
It yearns to be known, recognized, and understood.
It begs forgiveness, while refusing to forgive.
What a gentle nuance, this thing we call an inner life,
      what an exquisite gift.
It pushes and pulls at us like a toddler with places to go.
At times it pains me to look inside
And yet within, I hold the looking glass to worlds of splendor.

SEARCHING FOR MEANING

Socrates taught, "The unexamined life is not worth living."

I have struggled for the right image to describe the quest for meaning in our lives. Is it a journey, a path one takes, a perpetual search? Is it an extending outward or upward into the spiritual and rational landscape? Or is it a deepening, a digging for untapped sweet water which, at its source, nourishes all aspects of my being? To find meaning, do I climb Jacob's ladder with angels beckoning me to the next rung, or do I bend over Miriam's well, dark and deep and mysterious? To find the meaning of it all, must I journey forth or dig deep? Do I listen for answers, or do I search out truths that reconcile the paradoxes that madden us all?

For years I have told the following parable; today I begin to understand it.

> A father and his son, traveling together in a wagon, came to the edge of the forest. Some bushes thick with berries caught the child's eye.
>
> "Father," he asked, "may we stop awhile so that I may pick some berries?"
>
> The father was anxious to complete his journey, but he did not have it in his heart to refuse the boy's request. The wagon was called to a halt, and the son alighted to pick the berries. After a while, the father wanted to continue on his

way. But his son had become so engrossed in berry-picking that he could not bring himself to leave the forest.

"Son," cried the father, "we cannot stay here all day! We must continue the journey!"

Even his father's pleas were not enough to lure the boy away. What could the father do? Surely he loved his son no less for acting so childishly. He would not think of leaving him behind—but he really did have to get going on his journey.

Finally he called out: "You may pick your berries for a while longer, but be sure that you are still able to find me, for I shall start moving slowly along the road. As you work, call out 'Father, Father,' every few minutes, and I shall answer you. As long as you can hear my voice, know that I am still nearby. But as soon as you can no longer hear my answer, know that you are lost, and run with all your strength to find me!"[1]

This parable has many meanings on many levels. But what I understand today is the tension between the journey and the contemplative moment. The father is right. Meaning is to be discovered down the many paths our journey takes us. And the son is right. The beauty and meaning in the moment offer us sweetness and unexpected joy. So we pause and journey, pause and journey, all the while calling out to God, so as not to be lost forever in the woods. We call out and listen for a reply not in the form of a voice but in an acknowledgment of sorts, through a deep knowing that all is as it should be.

Hillel, a rabbi of the first century, taught, "Do not separate yourself from the community. Do not be certain of yourself until the day of your death. Do not judge another until you are in his place. Do not say, 'When I have time I will study,' lest you never have the time."[2]

Perhaps meaning is found in the tension between the world within and the world without. Meaning is found in the tension between self-reflection and relationship. It is found in the correlation between contemplation and practice. Meaning resides in the tender awareness of the connection between self and God, *ben adam l'maqom*, and between you and me, *ben adam l'havero*.

There is a danger that introspection may lead to self-absorption and even arrogance. I must not withdraw from the society of my contemporaries. I must not judge another's path. I must not think that any answer I possess is Ultimate Truth; it is only what occurs to me at the moment as a result of study and contemplation. For if I do, then the meaning of my life will become elusive and deceptive. What I believe to be true must be based on the wisdom of those who came before me, and it must result in actions that bring to the world the highest of ideals, such as love, peace, confidence.

So I dig to reach the sweet waters in the well of my being. I stretch to climb another rung toward understanding. I reach across an unnamed divide to tend to another's pain and soothe a stranger's fear. The search for meaning is hard work. It is to wonder and to do; it is to question and to practice. The integration of all aspects of self, the physical, emotional, spiritual and rational, brings the spine of my being into alignment. It brings integrity.

SHEMA: LISTENING IS THE LANGUAGE OF THE SOUL

Shema Yisrael, "Hear O Israel:" a simple verse from the Book of Deuteronomy that is quoted in the Gospel according to Mark and written in several places in every Jewish prayer book. "The watchword of our faith," the rabbis of the modern era tell us as their booming voices resound from the earth to the heavens and back again. Some rise to say it, others stay seated, some cover their eyes and sing it aloud, others say it softly under their breath. We say it when we wake, we say it before we sleep, and we say it at the bed of the dying.

Shema Yisrael, "Hear O Israel." "What is so important? What do You want me to hear?" I wondered as a child. "Tell me," I would whisper to the Invisible. "I am listening." And I was. I was listening for an insistent chatter not easily detected. I listened in ways not taught to me in school. I listened as a child does, lying in bed, late at night, in the foreboding quiet of the dark home. The house would sigh and moan and shift, distracting my late-night calm just enough to put me slightly on edge. The shadows seemed to breathe and float, especially in corners or open closets.

There, eyes open, staring into the darkness, my imagination was sharp. I drifted between waking and sleep while dream and vision and a wild hope swirled around my heart. *Listen and remember that all is possible, even likely,* I seemed to hear. The darkness was filled with God whispers, teaching me to understand what I was learning to hear.

Shema Yisrael, "Hear O Israel." It used to be easier to listen. As a child I did not silence the silence with the noise of the world and the wailing of my fears. It is where I played, where I imagined worlds of great and noble wonder; it was where I was at my best.

In Hebrew the word for meaning is *mashmaut*. The origin of this word is the root "to hear." It seems that meaning is to be listened for. And yet when Abraham and Sarah needed to understand the simple yet complex voice of the Invisible One, they journeyed to Beer Sheba, the land of the desert, a wilderness compared to their native Mesopotamia. Apparently the listening was better in the emptiness. Seeking, listening. Searching, hearing.

That is why, perhaps, *Shema Yisrael*, "Hear O Israel," is a command. We must hear, as if without that command we would be in danger of growing up and forgetting how. We forget because to a large extent we are victims of the Age of Reason—a philosophy of previous centuries in which all human activity was judged by its logic and scientific thinking. All that was rational was considered good and true. Irrational thought or behavior became inferior. Think of the criticism you have encountered for illogical thinking, for being too emotional.

But God is not rational. Goodness, beauty, love are not experienced by reason. Divine stirrings do not reside in the realm of logic. We have forgotten how to listen because listening has lost its value in our world. To be busy is to be productive. To be active is be healthy. To have things of import to do is to prove that you are indeed important.

I believe, as do others, that the human condition is composed of at least four aspects. We are intellectual, emotional/psychological, physical, and spiritual. The rational world is where the intellect is important. From a young age, intellectual capacity is encouraged and nurtured. We are urged to get good grades, read before we sleep, go to college. We are primed to be reasonable. "Smart" is mostly defined as a sharpness of intellect.

But we are also emotional and psychological beings. At least since the days of Freud, we know that we have an emotional life and are urged to be in touch with it while somehow keeping it in check. We either do our psychological work or not, and we can identify those who are "emotionally available," "hung up," or "stable."

And we are physical beings. We know that we must tend to our bodies, exercise and eat well, and when we don't—well, then it becomes a psychological issue. We also know that to live in this world we must physically engage. Particularly in Judaism, ethics is a physical activity. We must "do" good deeds. We must give to those in need, we must fight for those who are weak, we must embrace those who are in pain. Judaism is in part physical, it is what we do, and it is an activity of the body as well as the mind.

But we are also spiritual beings. We are created in the image of God. We have at our core a soul, which allows us access to the spiritual world. Since the Age of Reason, this aspect of self has been allowed to atrophy. The spirit speaks through the intuitive, not the logical, and so it is deemed inferior.

Gregg Levoy writes:

> The door will be barred to us if we attempt to cross by way of reason. No amount of intellectual authority, arrogant confidence, name dropping, or ego and ambition pounding at the door demanding to be admitted will allow us passage. Beyond a certain point, faith is the magic lamp and humility the abracadabra. Faith begins, if it begins at all, where knowledge leaves off. Even scientists will admit that they do all the homework they can but eventually rely on an intuitive leap. They call it informed intuition.[3]

We still live in the shadow of the Age of Reason. We may have passed through the Industrial Revolution, the Space Age, the Age of Technology, the Postmodern Era, but spiritually we got lost in the Age of Reason. It is a time when anything of value is measured by the extent to which it is rational, reasonable, and even progressive. Matters of the spirit fight with what we believe to be reasonable. The ultimate insult, mostly directed toward women, is that they are too emotional. That breaks the rules of the Age. To "hear" we need to suspend reason, and that too breaks the rules. So for decades we forgot how to be "trans-rational."

One late afternoon I entered my teenage daughter's room without knocking. I like to do this because I can catch a glimpse of her before she knows she is being seen. These moments are like the days when I watched her as a baby; she was unaware of anything but her own world, and I was in constant awe. Talia has never scolded me for this intrusion into her privacy, so until she does I push open the door, slowly, without knocking, to find her as she is, in her own world. This particular afternoon, she was curled up in her reading chair staring out the window.

"What are you doing?" I asked.

"Nothing," she answered.

"Don't you have homework to do?" I said.

"Yup," she answered.

"Have you studied for your test yet?" I asked.

"Nope," she answered.

"So what are you doing?" I asked again.

"I'm thinking," she said, unashamed. "First I'll think a while, then I'll do my work."

"Oh," I said, and turned around, gently closing the door behind me.

Thinking, listening to the sweet nothings of the universe, deepening, contemplating the next step my spirit is to take, all lead me a bit closer to a great understanding.

We as adults have for the most part stopped listening. That is why we believe that there is nothing to hear. All perceived information is information of the ears and mind and chatter of the physical world. I am commanded to hear, to listen for the quiet that I once understood. We forget how to listen, though according to the verse, we must remember how.

———— ～～ ⁄

Two weeks ago, silence was imposed on me in the most dramatic way. It reminded me that I had forgotten to enter solitude and be quiet for a prolonged while. It began on the drive home from the city to my suburban home during what had been an ordinary busy, rainy day. I was lulled by slow traffic, the atonal music of tapping rain and squeaky windshield wipers, gray skies, and a stagnant sense of time.

I was bored and impatient, so I decided to call my friend Rachel on my cell phone. We chatted for a moment or two, then she put me on hold to take another call. "It was Jonah," she said when she returned. Jonah was her eleven-year-old son, who was in my daughter's class at school. "Jonah said there was a horrible storm and a tree fell on our house. He told me to wait to come home until it passed." We commented on how sweet it was that he was concerned, and I said, "It's not raining too badly here. Are you worried? I could swing by on my way home." "No," she said. "The babysitter is there, and I'm heading home now."

As soon as we'd hung up I got another call, this time from my older daughter. "There's a really bad storm here, and Arna called wondering why the kids were forty minutes late coming home in the carpool." I hung up with Talia and called Arna. She was very upset. She had been driving, and a tree nearly hit her car. The wind rocked her Suburban and she felt as if it might overturn. She turned around and made it home to find a hundred-year-old tree on her roof. The kids were very late; wasn't my husband driving the carpool home? I told her that I was stuck in traffic and would call her if I heard anything.

The traffic was thickening and slowing to a crawl as I continued to make my way home. I glanced at the clock. The normal forty-five-minute ride had become an hour and a half with no end in sight. I looked up at the skies, or perhaps I was looking at the

heavens. But all I saw was a normal steady rain, no storm, no fun-
nel cloud, and no angels signaling to me that all was well. I felt my
breathing tighten to the beat of the wipers.

The phone rang, and I jumped in my seat. My hands gripped the
steering wheel. It was Shiri. Thank God, they're home, I whispered
out loud to the Invisible One. "Mom, it was horrible. We were
waiting for carpool, and all of a sudden a great wind came from all
directions. The kids had to hold the railings so as not to fly away.
The teachers pushed us back in the building, and water came
between the inner and outer doors so we couldn't get out. The
lights went out and the alarm sounded and the teachers yelled for
us to line up against the walls and cover our heads. I started to cry,
and Ellen [Arna's daughter] covered my head with her arms and
held me close. I was so scared I was shaking. Suddenly Daddy was
there and he seemed calm, so I calmed down a little." Ezra, my
husband, was in the school that day, substituting.

All I could say was, "Oh, my God," and I meant every word.
"Put Daddy on." Ezra confirmed all that Shiri said. He told me that
the condition of the roads was awful. There were trees and parts of
roofs everywhere.

At that point I was about fifteen miles from home. I looked at
the sky. Nothing but a sprinkle. It took me another hour to drive
those fifteen miles. As I neared my house, I felt as if I had entered
a war zone. Trees, branches, and downed wires were lying across
the street, in the yards, or on top of houses. Leaves were plastered
to cars by some mighty force. All of us on the road were headed in
one direction, the direction of our homes, to see the damage,
check loved ones, take shelter, take stock.

I missed the turn onto my street. The usual landmarks were on
their sides, directing me to places unknown. I turned around a few
times, wandering, trying to find my way. Then, finally, I was home.
We were OK. The family was all there, whole, fine. The house was
standing, undamaged, fine. The electricity was out. No light, no heat,
no oven, no stove. Ezra and I gathered all the candles, batteries,

matches, and flashlights and put them in the center of the kitchen table. The rain had stopped, but the clouds and wind still threatened. The sun was setting fast. We quickly took advantage of the remaining light to make dinner: tuna fish with low-fat mayonnaise, salad with a lemon dressing, and mashed avocado with a bit of salt and allspice—so ordinary it was odd.

After dinner I began to pace. What do we do now? Too soon to light candles, too early to go to bed. I decided to take a walk and check in on the neighbors. The neighborhood was in ruins: mighty trees snapped in half, bark peeled from the branches. People out on the street were telling the story over and over again. What was it? A tornado, heavy winds? The insurance people would call it an act of God. Apparently it was what meteorologists call a microburst.

A dark, cold night gave way to a sunny day and a flooded basement. I sent my family out to a museum to escape the damp oddness of home, and I stayed alone all day begging for plumbers to come, and then waiting for them, while staring at the rising water in my basement and pacing from room to room.

I spent the day twitching from the silence.

No television, no radio, no symphonic hum from a working home. Such quiet turns up the volume in your head. Internal voices shout in fear and self-doubt, memories return with their insistent chatter; thoughts recede into a kind of dumb numbness. It's enough to drive you mad.

And there was nothing I could do about it. All of the noise-makers I depended upon had vanished with the wind. Now what? I sat in my grandmother's chair, the chair I used to curl up in as a child when I wanted to read or just think. I tried to remember her smell and the softness of her skin. I looked out the window at the beauty of a world that had survived a storm. The colors were sharp, the sun warm, the wind oddly gentle. I began to think, then ponder, then breathe, and then, finally, I began to listen to the stillness.

The storm we experienced was violent, dramatic, frightening. The truth is that we live a great deal of our lives as if we are living in or running from a whirlwind. We chase life, filling our days with noise, obligation, doing, as if a great storm or worse is approaching and we must respond.

It has been said of the great rabbi of our generation, W. Gunther Plaut, that when he was young and serving a major congregation, he instructed his secretary that for the first four hours of every day she was to tell people who called, "The rabbi can't speak with you now, he's thinking."

This caused great anger and controversy in the congregation and finally reached the board of directors of the synagogue. They insisted that he be more responsive to his congregation and stop his secretary from saying such a thing. The next day he went to his study in the synagogue and told his secretary that for the first four hours of the day she was still not to pass him phone calls but to respond, "The rabbi can't talk right now, he is busy." The controversy settled, he continued to study and think, and he eventually wrote a commentary for the Torah that is used by Reform synagogues throughout the country. His congregation thought that he was very busy, and he enjoyed a long career in the synagogue.

It is socially acceptable to be busy; it is not acceptable to be still in thought and contemplation. But what if there were space for the quiet, the stillness, the opposite of the frantic run to finish? Just a bit of time spent in reflection, in solitude, could be the passageway to greatness. You would become acquainted with your thoughts, your dreams, your wisdom, the wisdom of the universe. Through quiet you can reach a certain spiritual depth.

Quiet, stillness, solitude are the sounds of God's presence. It is the sound of the horizon on fire when the sun is going down and the moon is rising. It is the sound of snow falling for the first time, a bit too early in November. It is the sound of a baby growing inside its mother's soft womb. It is the sound I was able to hear in my home because the hum of electricity was silenced. "Crystal

Silence,"[4] the jazz artist Chick Corea called his piece, in which the slow notes of a clarinet accented with bells transport you elsewhere. Silence that leads you to the clarity that the spiritual universe indeed communicates, in whispers so subtle that one must learn to listen all over again.

When the noisy imposition of the outside world is suddenly silenced, an inner cave can be discovered. God is like the great caverns of the world, where waters rush into deep crevasses creating places of cool beauty, dark and yet safe. And so, we are taught, an angel of God touched Elijah the Prophet at the entrance to the cave. God is best experienced when it is quiet enough to hear the soul touched by the stillness of its passing. "Who has seen the wind?" Christina Rossetti whispers. "Neither you nor I. But when the trees bow down their heads, the wind is passing by."[5]

To be in touch with God, with ultimate beauty and goodness, with the divine will, with the messages of the spirit, we must make room for the solitude that allows a spiritual silence to resound. If God is silent, perhaps you haven't learned how to listen. But if God is experienced as silence, then you have heard loud and clear. The storm forced me to sit and listen, but the truth is that I am at my best, most spiritually centered, when I create the emotional space for solitude.

Harmonizing rational thought with the beats of your heart and soul, allowing for silence by transcending the noise of the world, is like letting powerful and forceful waters rush through you, fashioning a hollow where God can reside.

Words are the language of the mind; silence is the language of the spirit. Sometimes to hear the language of the spirit, we must silence the language of the mind.

I learned to silence my mind on a hill in Wisconsin that slopes gently toward Lac La Belle. It was a trick I had discovered while I studied English literature at Towson State University in Maryland. At the edge of the campus, past the farthest parking lot, there was a hill, rather steep, very green and manicured. At the top of the hill there was a fence, a white picket fence like one in a Mark Twain story. But this fence was a boundary, a border between the university and a private institution for the mentally ill called Shepherd Pratt.

At night, when the stars were plentiful, I would climb this hill with my friend Tom. We'd go as far toward the fence as we felt was reasonable and safe. We would lie on our backs, with our heads pointing down the hill, and stare up at the sky. Stars exploded against a black velvet canopy. Stars with a red hue, stars that flickered ever so slightly, stars that made you squint into the darkness, not sure that they were really there, stars that ruled, larger, more solid than the others. Stars that formed patterns like the Little Dipper and Orion's Belt. Stars that defied pattern, random points of light scattered like dreams, like the thoughts of a seven-year-old child.

I loved this spot, the perspective it gave, the lights, the darkness, the upside-down rush of blood to my brain. "You can see Akron from here," Tom would say, imagining the stars to be the lights of a Midwestern town. But I saw eternity peeking through holes of light in a curtain of darkness, winking its eye knowingly. I was not yet twenty, and it seemed to me that the line between enlightenment and insanity was only as strong as a freshly painted picket fence.

So here I am, nearly thirty years later. Not especially insane, not particularly enlightened, most definitely searching. The summer sun in Wisconsin has been fickle, cooler than usual, all too ready to give way to clouds and rain. But today it shines, and today I am in search of a quiet grounding. On the hill sloping toward the lake, I lie backwards with my beginning Hebrew class. The sun is hot bright pink through our eyelids. "You can see Akron from here," I tell them. "Where's Akron?" they ask. "Just lie here, feel the heat of the sun, listen to the beating of your heart."

As I teach them the words for sun, hot, clouds in Hebrew, I realize that the fence marks a different boundary at this stage of my life. There is a line between sacred and profane, between noise and

God's quiet, between filling up with the world and filling up with the universe. I found my spirit on the hill in Wisconsin, hearing my heartbeat, pressing my back to the ground.

If you want moments of holiness, if you desire to feel God's presence, you must create the quiet that will allow the Divine to be experienced.

This is why the word *shema* is an imperative.

YISRAEL: STRUGGLING WITH REALITY

It is not easy to quiet the mind and open the soul. It is not easy to listen for God. The truth is, it is not easy to live. Life is so often a struggle with unseen forces, a wrestling with people, with circumstances, with inner demons, with angels. And so as we utter the next word in this verse from Deuteronomy, we acknowledge that it is a struggle to listen, to hear. *Yisrael* means one who struggles with God. How many times will we recount the renaming of our patriarch Jacob who struggled with a stranger, an angel of God, in the middle of the night? Like children who look at a family album, we seem to say, "Tell me the story again. How did we become the people of Israel, the great strugglers?"

It was in the middle of a dark night, on the bank of the River Jabbok, that our father, Jacob, had an encounter.

> Jacob was alone. A man wrestled with him until the break of dawn. When he saw that he had not prevailed against him, he wrenched Jacob's hip at the socket, so that the socket of his hip was strained as he wrestled with him. Then he said, "Let me go, for the dawn is breaking." But he answered, "I will not let you go, unless you bless me." Said the other, "What is your name?" He replied, "Jacob." He said, "Your name shall no longer be Jacob, but Israel, for you have wrestled with Beings Divine and human and have prevailed." Jacob asked, "Tell me your name." But he said, "You must not ask my name!" and he left him there.[6]

And so we tell the story of how Jacob wrestled with a stranger, some say an Angel of God, and how he was wounded from the fight. And we learn that sometimes when we wrestle with God, when we shake our fists at the heavens yelling "What was that about?" sometimes we are wounded. In the name of God people are killed, lives destroyed. People are in pain and sometimes lives are destroyed.

It is hard to suffer. It is even harder to love those who suffer. It is maddening to watch those who are insane with misled religious zeal destroy without sense or reason. Life challenges our sense of fairness, justice, and basic right. It simply is not right that a young mother die of breast cancer. It is not right that her teenage children are thrown into a world where spiritual and emotional survival are an overwhelming challenge. It is not right that her husband should wander through life not finding love and peace for years after her death.

God-listening is a tricky business fraught with dangers. To be a person of faith takes courage and a limber sense of reason. Belief in God and the fundamental goodness of life often contrasts sharply with the events of our lives. Jacob teaches us that if we wrestle with God, we are in good company, for we are the children of Israel.

Today the sunlight invited me to walk a slow uncharted mile where the only sound I heard was the soft crackle of my step against the autumn leaves. My mind wandered along with my path until I had a thought that soon became louder than any other sound and repeated itself over and over. I thought: "I don't believe that God exists in theoretical discourse or philosophical proofs. Rather, God is experienced, if allowed, in the soft spots of the human heart. Softness that sometimes hurts like a bruise or an open wound and sometimes is so soft that you feel as if you are warmed by fine cashmere."

Soft spots. The soul. The spirit of a human life. The Divine within. All are words and phrases describing a sense we have that there must be more than the physical world, more than the body and even the mind. These words describe the struggle we have to discover meaning and purpose, the struggle we have to connect with the divine intention for our lives. I believe that God can be experienced in that internal spot, which is ever so soft and vulnerable.

I don't remember meeting Jared. Apparently I did, though. I had conducted the funeral of his uncle, and after it was over, Jared, who was twenty-one years old, took his parents aside and said, "This is what I want when I die." They tried to silence him and he said, "No, listen. When I die I want a funeral just like this." So when he was hit and instantly killed by a car crossing Wacker Drive in downtown Chicago, his family called me.

I went to his parents' small apartment. His mother wailed and moaned, her arms and face pointing toward the heavens. She kept saying, "My angel, my angel, he's now my angel." His father was pale and silent as if he'd been holding his breath for hours. His friends, handsome, young, and strong, paced in utter confusion and fear. The soft spot in all of us was bleeding. No book, no class, no philosophical discourse can teach you how to help a family survive the death of a twenty-one-year-old. No theoretical argument can explain why he died.

The next day, as I walked past my secretary's desk on my way to conduct the funeral, she stopped me and said I had to take a phone call. I looked at my watch and began to say no, but she insisted. The caller identified himself as Greg Finnegan. "I read in the paper that you are doing Jared's funeral. I wish I could come.... I just can't seem to.... Just do me a favor. Tell his parents that I was there when he died. I too was crossing the street, and I heard the car hit him. I'm a former Marine, and I know what death looks like. Tell them that he didn't suffer. Tell them that I held him in my arms and said a prayer as he died. Just tell them that he wasn't alone."

Nearly a year after the funeral, Jared's parents called me. "We want to meet Finnegan," said the father. "We just can't make the call ourselves. This is too hard, but he was the last to see Jared alive. We have to talk with him. Can you arrange a meeting?"

Though I had since changed jobs and many of my files were still in boxes, I still had Finnegan's phone number, written in my former secretary's handwriting. I arranged the meeting. It was Shabbat afternoon, early in the fall, and the only sound I heard as I approached my office was the soft crackle of my step against the autumn leaves.

The two couples met, Finnegan and his wife, Jared's mother and father. Unable even to say "How do you do," they embraced one another for quite a while and cried softly. Finally we sat down, and they talked. First about what happened, then about how the police mishandled the case against the woman who was driving, and then slowly about themselves. The more Finnegan spoke about himself and his feelings since the accident, the more I felt that though none of us should ever lose a child, if we did, it should be in the arms of a man like Finnegan.

As the conversation came to an end, Jared's mother pulled out a package wrapped in pretty paper and gave it to him. He opened it, and we saw a large sun made out of cut glass and metal with a place for a candle at its base. Jared's mother said, "Jared's symbol was the sun. He had one tattooed on his back. Jared's memory should be the light that was his life, not the tragedy that was his death. I bought one of these for myself and one for you because I was there when he came into this world, and you were there when he left. I want to know that when I light my candle and think of the legacy of light that he has left, that you are doing the same."

Why did Jared die so young? I don't know. In fact, if anyone tries to give you an answer, turn around and walk away. It defies rational understanding. Where was God when he died? God was in the embracing arms of a stranger, in the healing conversation between this stranger and Jared's parents. In fact, God is in the softness of my tears as I write their story.

Jared's story touches us because it is sad, but also because it allows us to face the struggle for spiritual equilibrium. Jared, even in his death, is a powerful teacher. His mother tells me that she hears his voice from the heavens saying, "Breathe, live, do not let life defeat you."

Why is it that the tenacity of the human spirit, the overwhelming beauty of nature, the miracle of birth, the simple joy of first snow falling silently at midnight are not enough to sustain a belief in God? Tragedy and sadness seem to have more force and power and often banish faith and belief for generations. This is why I am drawn to loss and sadness—to understand the power they have to break or strengthen faith, to bear witness to those who have experienced the unthinkable and yet whose faith has survived.

I feel compelled to tell you their stories. For you ask, so very often with tears in your eyes and fear in your hearts, where was God when my mother suffered with cancer? Where is God in the silent boredom of my life? Where was God during the Holocaust? It's not for me to answer. I listen to you, the survivors. Because ultimately you are right: If your faith in God cannot sustain you in your pain, who needs it?

How wise and prophetic was the choice to name the Jewish state *Israel*. It is truly a place where Jacob's nighttime struggles are felt during every waking hour.

The ride to my home in northern Jerusalem ascended the mountain just to the left of Mount Scopus. Turning sharply left, just before you would make your descent to the Dead Sea, I would pass on my right the ancient village of Anatot, the home of the prophet Jeremiah. Today, however, Anatot is called Anata. It is a Palestinian refugee camp, which from the days of the Intifada can at times be violent. At the intersection there is a hill where Arab children stand and throw rocks and Molotov cocktails at the motorists below.

So every day, when I took my daughter Talia home from preschool at Beit Shmuel, I would turn this corner and have this series of thoughts: *I can't believe I live in the neighborhood of Jeremiah the prophet.... Is it safer for me to put Talia in a car seat, lest, God forbid, we have an accident, or is it safer to keep her out of the seat, lest I need to quickly get her out of the car in the case of a Molotov cocktail?*

Do you want to know what is most horrifying to me today? Not that I had the thought, but rather, how casual and unalarming the thought was. On some level, Israel is used to being Israel, one who struggles with unseen forces. Though I never voiced these thoughts to my daughter, one day not too long after a terrorist attack on a Jerusalem bus, we turned that very same corner and I heard my daughter softly singing to herself, safely buckled in her seat. I strained to hear what nursery rhyme she learned in school; was it "Yonatan HaKatan" ("Jonathan the Small and Rambunctious Boy") or "Ima Yikara Li, Yikara" ("My Mother Is Very Dear to Me") my personal favorite? But it was neither. What I heard was the *nusach*, the chant, from the morning prayers.

I sat up in my seat, proud of the Jewish education the Israeli Reform Movement was giving to my daughter. As I listened, I realized Talia was making up her own blessings to the *nusach*. *Baruch Ata Adonai*, that I should eat all my vegetables. *Baruch Ata Adonai*, that we should be healthy and not be killed. Five years old and Talia understood as Jacob did: life is a struggle.

Listening is hard. Living a life that includes the demands and commands of the spiritual world is a challenge. It is a struggle to reconcile reality with the tender yearning and dreams of the heart. This world that we have created, this life that we have been granted, confronts us with dramatic struggles on a regular basis. Perhaps that's really the reason we have stopped listening: it is too much of a struggle. And yet, with the spiritual world muted, we become strangers to meaning and purpose. *Shema Yisrael*: Hear, you strugglers with God.

ADONAI ELOHEINU ADONAI ECHAD: ALL IS ONE

All the world, the world we know and the world we believe to be, the natural world and the spiritual world, the world of our lives and the worlds of others' lives, the world in our minds and the world in our souls, the world we have created and the world that was created for us. All this and more is One.

The third word in the Deuteronomy verse is *YHVH*. The word *YHVH* is pronounced as "Adonai," which means "my Lord." But that is not the true pronunciation of the word. The true pronunciation was lost with the destruction of the Temple in Jerusalem in the year 70 C.E. It was always a secret word, mysterious and powerful. The high priest in the Holy of Holies could say it only on Yom Kippur. With the destruction of the Temple and therefore the end of the priesthood, the magic of the word has been lost. If we look at the root, we see that it is derived from the verb "to be." It is a strange form of this verb, defying grammar, gender, and tense.[7]

A possible translation of this name for God is "beingness," completing the verse: "Hear, you strugglers with God, there is a Beingness in the universe, which we call our God; this Beingness is a great Oneness."

I am commanded to hear that there is no true separation, only the one created by my struggles, my ego, my fears. The angels who visit me in the night are trying to reveal to my soul that I am a part of a reality created from the beginning of time. There is a Oneness in the world. I call it God, and being created in that

image, I am invited to live in the shadow of Its wings. Hear O
Israel, God is One. All is One.

Just how must we "be" to be in the image of the Great Oneness?

Once Rabbi Eisig of Ziditzov traveled to a village where only
one poor Jew lived. The poor man took him in, fed him, pre-
pared a bed for him. But all the while he sighed.

"Why do you sigh?" Rabbi Eisig asked him.

"Because I cannot show you the honor you deserve,"
replied the poor man.

Touched by the man's generosity of heart, the rabbi gave
him his blessing and departed the next day.

From that moment on, the poor man's fortunes began to
rise until he became the wealthiest man in the area. So many
beggars came to his door that he hired a guard to keep them
away. He gained a reputation as a heartless miser.

After a time, Rabbi Eisig returned to the village and
called at the Jew's house, but the guard turned him away.

"My master is meeting with a very important person,"
announced the guard gruffly.

"Tell your master," replied Rabbi Eisig, "that I am the
one responsible for all his wealth."

The guard went inside and soon returned with permis-
sion for Rabbi Eisig to enter. He led the rabbi into a magnificent parlor and told him to wait there. After a long time, his
host entered the room and spoke a few curt words to him. It
was obvious that he was eager for the rabbi to leave.

"Look through that window," Rabbi Eisig said to him.
"What do you see?"

"People going about their business," replied his host.

Then the rabbi said, "Look in the mirror. Now what do
you see?"

"Only myself," answered the rich man.

"Both the window and the mirror are made of glass,"
said Rabbi Eisig. "But through one you can see others and

through the other, only yourself. The only difference between them is a gilt coating. It is time to scratch off the gilt."

Immediately grasping the rabbi's meaning, the rich man cried, "Only leave me my wealth, and I promise to change my ways!"

And true to his word, he made true repentance and never again turned away a needy soul from his door.[8]

I look to the many mirrors of my life. The one on the wall reveals my face. It is easily changed or enhanced or even manipulated. I can smile or frown, I can stare or put on makeup to cover the lines, I can turn away and choose not to look at all. But there are other mirrors that are harder to turn away from. There is the mirror in the eyes of those who know me, those who love me and those who don't, those who trust me and those who don't, those who fear me and those who set me apart. All these mirrors reflect some deeper truth and are not easily fooled.

The mirror in the eyes of those who love me reflect my beauty, the goodness of who I yearn to be; they reflect the truth of my higher self. And the mirror in the eyes of those who despise me reflect my fear, the many emotions that separate me from a sense of connectedness. I see in their look my guilt, my anger, and my resentment. They are the faithful measure of my refusal to forgive and my inability to love and my difficulty in reflecting back to them their beauty, from the mirror of my eyes. They mirror the separation I feel.

On the second day of our car trip from Denver to Chicago, the kids were unusually quiet in the back seat. Ilan was playing with his action figures in the continual battle to save the world from evil, Talia was dreaming to the beat of some secret music that only she could hear, and Shiri was staring out the window. Suddenly, quite unrelated to anything I could fathom, Shiri asked, "Why are people sometimes mean to one another?"

"Because they are frightened and hurt so they lash out in a mean way," I answered.

"So why are we called man*kind?*" she asked.

I looked in the rearview mirror. She was gazing out the window with a blank stare. "Because we're all alike," I answered. "Basically, we're all the same."

In the underbelly of O'Hare Airport, the hallways and byways that lead to elevators and escalators, I heard the sound of a saxophone echoing off the concrete walls. It was a music man, playing jazz, and he played it as if he meant it. I stopped to find a dollar to give him, fumbling in my pockets for the change I keep handy for such occasions. Along came a man, a stranger out of nowhere, and threw a couple of coins in the musician's case. The stranger said, "I saw you were kind to that family a while ago. That was nice of you."

"It was nothing," the music man said. I looked at him, still searching for my coins.

"So you're kind, are you?" I asked

"Yes, I am," he said.

"That's nice," I said. "The world needs a bit of kindness."

"There are a lot of us scattered about all over. You just have to find them," he said.

I found four quarters and a penny, threw them into his saxophone case, and went on my way as he played another tune.

That veil we place between ourselves and another is thin. How thick is the veil we place between the Divine and ourselves! I want to understand that separation is a psychological state and that my soul yearns for oneness. To understand that I am a part of all things, that my life can be a channel for the Spirit of the Universe. *Use me, God. Let Your Will flow into and through me as I try to serve with integrity.* To be in service to God is to realize that there is a loving force in the universe, and I must pull away the veil and allow that force to come through.

The prayers that come before and after the *Shema* both speak of love. The prayer before begins: *Ahava raba ahavtanu Adonai Eloheinu,* You love us, O God, with great abundant love. *Shema Yisrael,* Hear O Israel. What is it that we are supposed to hear? We are to hear that we are supported by great abundant love from the Spirit of the Universe, which is One and is all-pervasive. This love is different from emotional love. It is a love that connects to all that is essential and good at the core or the center of our being.

Mary Caroline Richards writes:

> How are we to transform ourselves into limber and soft organisms lying open to the world at the quick? By what process and what agency do we perform the Great Work, transforming lowly materials into gold? Love, like its counterpart Death, is yielding at the center. At the center love must live.
>
> One gives up all one has for this. This love that resides in the self, the self-love out of which all love pours. The fountain, the source. At the center. One gives up all the treasured sorrow and self-mistrust, all the precious loathing and suspicion, all the secret triumphs of withdrawal. One bends in the wind.
>
> There are many disciplines that strengthen one's athleticism for love. It takes all one's strength. And yet, it takes all one's weakness too. Sometimes it is only by having all one's so-called strength pulverized that one is weak enough, strong enough, to yield. Look at this flower. Look at this child. Look at this rock with lichen growing on it. Listen to this gull scream as he drops through the air to gobble the bread I throw and clumsily rights himself in the wind. Bear ye one another's burdens, the Lord said, and He was talking law.
>
> Love is not a doctrine. Peace is not an international agreement. Love and Peace are beings who live as possibilities in us.[9]

Love is a state of mind, a worldview, a knowing that all is connected and supported abundantly. Sometimes I divide the world into halves. Sometimes I see the world filled with people who think that there is always enough and those who believe that there is never enough. This worldview is never reflective of how much there really is. It cannot be measured in the bank accounts of the world or by the amount of stuff we have. Consider the attitude that says there is always room for one more, against the view that there will not be enough to go around. Or the one who buys another dress against the one who feels that yet another piece of clothing is wasteful. These two attitudes reflect an abundant worldview and a worldview of lack. Ultimately they sift away to two spiritual beliefs: one that we are supported by love abundantly, and the other that there is not enough love to go around.

Hear, you strugglers with God, you are a part of the Oneness in the universe and you are infinitely loved.

The prayer following the *Shema* begins, "And you shall love YHVH, your God, with all your heart, with all your soul, and with all your might." Having listened, knowing that we are loved, our only response is then to offer love in return. The center of this prayer is the phrase *v'shinatam l'vanecha*, translated usually as "You shall teach your children diligently" or "faithfully." But the word *v'shinatam* does not really mean "diligent" or "faithful"; rather, it means teaching by repetition. In this case, teaching over and over again: You are loved. You are loved. This, it seems, is the central teaching we should give our children, building for them a world-view of abundance.

We should teach our children, all children, that they are loved abundantly by a loving God who is the essence of the entire world and whose spark is deep in our souls.

How would your life have been different if your parents told you to look both ways before you cross the street and wash your hands before eating, and then, you are loved, you are loved? Put your napkin on your lap, and, by the way, you are loved by a loving God who supports you. With that understanding from my youngest years, I would be able to hear the spiritual chatter of the universe with greater ease and the mirrors in my life would, more often than not, reflect loveliness at its most basic.

We are taught: "In the beginning there was heaven and earth. The earth was unformed and void and darkness was on the face of the earth and chaos, and the spirit of God hovered over the deep. And God said let there be light and there was light." And there was light. Its origin is divine and elusive. This light is breathed into being and is beyond the cycles of creation. This light is different. It is of this world and yet not of this world. Perhaps it is yet another metaphor for God. Not at all a part of a world that is about to be created, but rather a consequence of birthing the world. Let creation begin with light. It is the banishment of eternal darkness, into the brilliant explosion of eternal light.

This was not the light of the sun and moon. They were created several days later. This was a different kind of light, a light that I have been seeking for decades now. I remember conversations with my physics teacher. "If we could grind the right lens, make the correct calculations, could we see the light from creation?" I would ask him, as he taught me physics during our mid-day private lessons. "Well, yes. I suppose so," he said. The rabbis concur, I told him. "What is the origin of this light? It is the essence of God, seen as a flowing gown casting its brilliance and glory for all time."[10]

Both Einstein and the rabbis of the early centuries agree that this light is eternal. My professor was intrigued, I was mystified. Never would I look at the Eternal Light glowing in all Jewish sanctuaries the same way again. Listening to the prayers, I stare above the Ark, the place where the Torah scrolls are kept, to find clues into the mystery. "Don't blow out the Sabbath lights," I would teach the children. They represent eternity, I would think to myself.

Drawn to this powerful metaphor, I began to seek the light within. Rashi, an eleventh-century French commentator of the Bible, comments on Genesis by saying that this early light of creation is the light of the righteous ones yet to come into being. So I believe that deep within my soul, the place where righteousness lives and goodness shines, there is a light that burns with an ancient glow. It is the light of the Divine Spirit, for we have been created in the image of God. It is a gift from creation. It serves as a lighthouse for goodness and beauty. To be in service to God is to be a beacon of light.

Rabbi Yaakov said that the light of the first day is seen by humanity for all time.[11]

So I search for the light, the unifying essence of all things. I ask to truly understand that the basis for knowing the Divine is knowing a deep spiritual love. I yearn to feel the Great Oneness. Oneness can be felt in prayer, while immersed in nature, in a moment of awe. Oneness can be felt when we remove the gilt, the separation between others and us. The Oneness can be felt in relationship with others or even with strangers. Tonight I light a candle, maybe two, to remind me that I am deeply connected to the origin of things, to remind me that though I struggle, I must learn to hear the commanding voice of God that bids me to join in the act of creation, every day, anew, in goodness and faith.

NOTICING THE INVISIBLE

Most things in life that are truly important are invisible, like kind-ness, love, dignity, peace. They are so invisible that we only notice them when they are gone. Many aspects of my life are invisible, like integrity, my true self, my dreams. They are never really noticed until they're gone. God is like that. God is invisible.

To live a life with meaning, you must notice the invisible.

One fall day I had a lesson in the invisible. I went with my friend Lisa to downtown Chicago to help her with a business mat-ter that she needed to attend to. I love Chicago, but at the time I had lived there for only two years, and the roads to the city always confused me. There is a lovely lakeside road that twists and turns, merges into other roads, disappears and reappears, and moves very fast. I'm never sure how I actually manage to stay on it; in fact, when I make the twenty-five-mile journey south to the city with-out getting lost, I consider it a miracle. So here we were going home on this fast-moving mysterious road when Lisa said, "Stop, we have to go to the Museum of Contemporary Art."

"What stop, Lisa? I can't stop, I'm on Lake Shore Drive being guided by the angels of destinations."

"No, really, we have to go to this museum." Now, my friend Lisa is not one to insist or impose herself on others. So I quickly made a left turn, and lo and behold I was on the street right in front of the museum. It was another miracle. I approached the intersection, which is in the heart of downtown Chicago, and I looked to my left and there was a parking space. Now that's a real miracle. We parked the car and started toward the steep white steps that ascend toward the museum. It was rather eerie. There was no one in sight, as if this little corner of the city had been deserted. We tried the doors of the museum and they were locked. It was Monday; the museum was closed.

Now—true story—at just the moment I had the thought, Why did God bring me to this place if not to see the museum? a woman appeared from nowhere. I will never forget what she looked like. She was a thin, pretty woman dressed in white jeans and a white T-shirt. She had a large straw bag over her shoulder. Her hair was pulled back in a neat ponytail, and her clear, beautiful skin was the color of chestnut. On her hip was perched a baby nearly two years old, also dressed in white, crying, her eyes filled with large tears and her small nose running.

The woman looked at us and said, "I mean you no harm, I really mean you no harm, but I need help. I just left my home, my husband is beating me up, and I'm afraid. I don't mean you no harm, but I need help. There is no room in the shelter near here. I called the shelter across town, but I have to get there in forty-five minutes before they close. I don't mean you no harm, but could you help me?"

I looked to my left, and there was a cab sitting right there. We put her in the cab and handed her a twenty-dollar bill. We asked the cab driver if that would cover it, and he said it probably would. We pulled out another twenty and gave it to her. The cab drove off, and we stood there in silence watching it fade into the distance. Finally my friend said to me, "You know what my husband is going to say? He's going to say that we were just taken for forty dollars. That she drives two blocks, pays the fare, and pockets the rest." I looked at my friend Lisa and said, "You know what I think? I think that she is a *lamed vavnik.*"

"*Lamed vavnik,* what's that?" Lisa asks.

"According to the Jewish mystical tradition, there are thirty-six righteous people who sustain the world. They are called *lamed vavniks*. The problem with these thirty-six is that they are not easily known. In fact, oftentimes they come in the guise of a beggar, and because we turn our backs on them, we delay redemption. I think that we just met a *lamed vavnik*, one of the thirty-six righteous who sustain the world."

Who was right? The truth is we don't know who was right. It is quite possible that she did pocket the remainder of the fare two blocks from us. It is also possible that she went to the shelter, and then left to go back to her husband. It is possible that she took our money and bought drugs or alcohol with it. It is possible that she stayed in the shelter, and now, because of our forty-dollar investment, she is starting a new life. It is possible that she went home to him and he beat her so badly that she lives in fear to this day.

It is also possible, I believe, that she was indeed a *lamed vavnik*. The real truth of this story is that we do not know what happened to this woman and her baby. The real truth of this story is what would have happened to me if I had walked away and not given to her when she said she was in need. What has happened to my soul those times that I have turned my back on someone in need?

The truth of this story lies in the spiritual law of giving and receiving. When I extend my hand to give, it is also extended and open to receive. This is what is meant by the phrase, "The world is sustained by acts of loving-kindness." The truth of this woman was unknown, and the reason or meaning in our encounter was quite invisible. It is so easy not to notice, to ignore, to walk by, to not look into her eyes, her fear, her baby's tears.

To live a life of meaning, you must practice seeing the invisible.

A story is told of Yossele the Miser. It seems that this very wealthy man refused to give away any of his wealth to the poor of the Ghetto Cracow. People hated him for his stinginess and the ugly manner in which he would deny them money. People would sneer at him, and children would throw stones in his direction.

One day word got out that Yossele was dying. The Burial Society came to see him and asked him for a thousand rubles before he died to feed their families. Yossele refused them in his typically ugly way, and they left him to die alone. After his death it took days for them to remove the body, for none felt the need to tend to him. Finally he was buried outside of town in an unmarked grave.

At the same time, a strange thing began to happen. The citizens of the town started to come to the rabbi and ask for money for Shabbat. The rabbi granted them what they needed, and then out of curiosity asked them why they had begun coming just now; what had they been doing up until that moment to sustain themselves? After some time, it became clear to the rabbi that Yossele, the despised miser, had secretly been giving *tzedakah* (money) to the poor just before the Sabbath.

The rabbi of the town was heartbroken. Yossele was the holiest man in town, and yet he lay buried alone outside the Jewish cemetery. The rabbi asked that his people fast and pray for Yossele's forgiveness so that he would receive a sign that they had been forgiven. The rabbi then had a vision that Yossele was in the Garden of Eden surrounded by righteous souls. Tell the people to go home, he said; there's no need to forgive them. "This is what I chose for myself: to have the privilege of giving as God gives, without anyone knowing."[12]

Most things in life that are truly important are invisible, like kindness, love, dignity, peace. When we give, the power is quite unseen; when we receive, so much of the impact is not apparently known. The forces at work in the spiritual world are often quiet and hidden.

The great Israeli poet Yehuda Amichai writes,

Bird tracks in the sand on the seashore
Like the handwriting of someone who jotted down
Words, names, numbers and places, so he would remember.
Bird tracks in the sand at night
Are still there in the daytime, though I've never seen
The bird that left them. That's the way it is
With God.[13]

With my eyes I see the tracks on the sand, but it's not my only means of sight. Turning inward and seeing with clarity, with internal vision, enables you to see beauty in ironic and unplanned moments or a simple expression of your highest dream. It is called insight. And when you get good at it, it's called enlightenment: an internal light that connects to the Source of all light. Watch with your eyes, search with your soul, and you too may discover the prints of a three-toed creature left in the sand in the middle of some night that you were sure was dreamless.

PASSION

Passion. The burning ember within your heart that warms you, sometimes a bit too much, glowing, not igniting into fire that destroys. The energy that fuels life, sustains it, gives it reason, makes it rhyme. Passion: a riddle that motivates you to take a journey of a thousand moments to find one answer. Pushing, pulling, tugging, dancing, leading you blindly down the path. A strong line that moors your aimlessness and yet also an unseen current that sends you adrift to uncharted waters.

Passion. The stuff that makes sense out of life. It is your reason for living, your gift from the divine spark of meaning and purpose. Passion. It is the relentless whisper that tells you who you really are, what you really care about, what you must give to the world at all costs. It is the whisper you are so often taught to ignore because it does not speak the language of profit. Rather it urges you, nudges you. It is constant and demands that you surrender to it. What is your passion? Don't be afraid to ask. Do not be afraid to answer.

The irises of the Gilboa Mountains are dark, dull purple with veins of black and a splash of inner white. They are large, and when the sun hits them just in the right way, they are translucent. They are rare and unique to the Gilboa Mountains, the mountains in the north of Israel where King Saul took his life by falling on his sword at the end of a difficult battle. The legend says that these mountains are essentially bald, barren of trees and foliage, because they still mourn the death of Israel's first king. They are bald except for scattered wildflowers and the irises, which have a two-week bloom in early spring, if all goes according to God's plan.

On my second date with the man I was to marry, I was invited to seek out the elusive iris. I was studying in Jerusalem and was introduced to him through mutual friends. As he was leaving my apartment he said, "Next week we are going to the Gilboa Mountains to see the irises. Want to come?"

"Sure." I was intrigued.

"I'll see you next Friday, then."

Ezra appeared at my apartment late Friday afternoon, as Jerusalem was winding down to a sweet hum preparing to welcome the Sabbath Queen. I threw my backpack in the back as I climbed into a small car, which was already crowded with his friends, whom I did not know. We drove. We drove as the sun set behind the quiet horizon of the Mediterranean Sea. His friends chattered in a language I was just beginning to understand. I thought I understood one of them to say that perhaps we were too late, that there had been a sighting two weeks ago and we might not find any irises left. They discussed that possibility for quite a while and lost me in the twirl of their accents. The radio was playing classic songs by Israel's most popular recording artists.

We drove. I looked out the window as the world darkened to a rose color, then blue, then purple, then shadow. I retreated into my own world, silent, feeling strange with these strangers, their strange language and the strange quest for the last seasonal remnants of a flower far on the top of a distant mountain.

We drove into the darkness and finally arrived at the foot of the mountain. We stayed at Yokniam, a *moshav* (village) offering shelter to travelers. We drank strong coffee sitting in front of the fire while they told stories of past excursions. I tried to listen, but mostly I waited for light to dawn on the valley below and peek around Mount Tabor, the mountain of Deborah, ancient Israel's poet-prophet.

Morning came, and we continued the drive up Mount Gilboa. We parked the car and started out on foot on its flat, wide, and rocky summit. We walked and walked, looking in crevasses for the elusive irises. We walked and searched and were about to give up when one of Ezra's friends called out to us. He had found one, no two, two irises that grew only on this near-naked mountain. There they were, majestically purple, a bit wrinkled at the tips, ready to fade from sight for the next pilgrim never to find. Ezra was in awe. He kept saying with great reverence, "It's so beautiful, look how beautiful."

I think back to that Shabbat afternoon and realize that we were truly engaged in holy activity. Though Ezra would not put it this way, as we searched for the last iris on Mount Gilboa, we actually searched for the great treasure that God plants in places all around to prove some divine truth. There was an irrational quality to our trip, as if we were on a holy pilgrimage.

I now have known Ezra for twenty years, and I realize that this is his passion: the quest for the details of the Land of Israel, its rocks and flowers, its hidden streams and underground wells, its mountains and valleys. To walk the land and feel its dust and sweat and years of promise and dreams—for this purpose he was born, and indeed Ezra is, by profession, a tour guide.

Passion is the unstoppable surge of energy that rushes through your soul revealing the divine reason for your life. It is not hard to find, though it is easy to lose. You lose touch because of years of people ignoring, criticizing, or rationalizing your passion right out of you. But it is there. It begs you to come hither and charts your course, if you let it.

Passion is mission, mission is purpose, purpose is meaning.

Rabbi Mordechai Joseph Leiner of Izbica defines passion as the way in which we express our love for God. He says that when we are spiritually immature, we do all the *mitzvot,* deeds commanded by God, with all our might. This is a phrase that refers to an unfocused zeal for performing every *mitzvah* possible. But, Rabbi Mordechai Joseph Leiner of Izbica says, as we deepen and season our spirit, we learn the gift of focus. We learn that we were created for a purpose, and that the one *mitzvah* that is our inheritance reveals our purpose.

What one *mitzvah*, godly deed, were you created to perform? It is written in *Midrash Tehillim*:

> When a person is asked in the World to Come: "What was your work?" and he answers, "I used to feed the hungry," it will be said to him, "This is the Gate of God, you who feed the hungry may enter." When a person answers, "I used to clothe the naked," it will be said to him, "This is the Gate of God, you who clothe the naked may enter." And similarly those who looked after orphans, who were involved in *tzedakah* [charitable acts] and performed deeds of loving-kindness.[14]

The Gates of Heaven are many; they are unlocked by our commitment and faithfulness to our passion, our mission.

As a rabbinic student I was taught that we all have one great sermon to give, and we will repeat it throughout our careers. This sounded odd at the time, and then I heard the following joke: There was a minister who gave a terrific sermon one Sunday morning; all the parishioners were very impressed. The following Sunday she rose and gave the same sermon. Her people were a bit confused but said nothing. The following week she gave the same sermon. This went on for the next several weeks. The board of directors met to discuss their options and finally decided that they would send one of the board to speak with her.

"Pastor," he began slowly, "you know how much respect we have for your work, compassion, and wisdom."

"Thank you," she said.

"Just one thing is beginning to alarm us."

"What is that?" she asked.

"Well, it seems you have been giving the same sermon over and over again for the past several weeks."

"Yes," she said.

"Well." He was getting impatient. "How long do you think you will repeat the same sermon?"

"Until you get it."

I believe, however, that my professor was telling us the opposite. We will give this one great sermon over and over in many guises until *we* get it. It seems that here is a message burning in our hearts, or maybe a question trying to be known. What question is your life trying to answer? What theme, constant pursuit, inconsolable itch motivates your life? Ponder that, and you engage in a search-and-find mission for the reason for your life.

We play so many roles in life that one could become dizzy from obligation. But in addition to our responsibilities and jobs, we are obligated to fulfill some great task in the world. A God who has implanted sparks of the Divine within calls us to greatness. There is a reason for our living, and that reason gives us unlimited energy and joy. Take it with you to the chores of your life.

By taking my current job, I was leaving the congregational rabbinate. Shiri had delighted in seeing me leading people in worship, telling stories to children, teaching, giving sermons, and performing life-cycle ceremonies. It gave her a sense of pride, I think. So when I took the job called "regional director," she asked maybe ten times, "So Mom, you're not going to be a rabbi any more, right?" Her question hurt me greatly and went straight to the doubts I was having in accepting this position. I had wanted to be a rabbi since I was a small child; was I betraying my calling? So each time Shiri asked, "So Mom, you're not going to be a rabbi anymore, right?" I answered the only way I could, by smiling, turning on my heel, and walking away.

Until one morning. We were alone at the kitchen table, and the sun was particularly bright and reflecting off the wood table, making Shiri squint. We were eating our breakfast of cereal and low-fat milk. I was listening to the clanging of the spoon against the glass bowl and the crunching and slurping of my nine-year-old. I was not particularly deep in thought. Suddenly Shiri asked again, "So Mom, I don't get what you're going to do. Aren't you going to be a rabbi anymore?" Her tenacity paid off. Her questioning had forced me to realize something I had never considered before.

"Shiri," I began, "people are called to do several things in life. Two of them are their job and their work. Your job is what you get paid to do, what your boss thinks is important, what your contract describes. But your work is what you have been given by God to do to change your little corner of the world. It is your passion, your reason for living. It is what you must do if you live a life of integrity. My job is that of regional director, but my *work* is to connect people with one another and with their faith in God. I will be taking my *work* with me to this new job."

The search for our passion is also the search for authenticity. When we ignore one, we by definition ignore the other. It takes courage, diligence, and often audacity to live by the command of your passion and in doing so be true to who you are. We define ourselves so often by what we do, or how we should be, and not by who we were meant to be.

"In the World to Come," taught Rabbi Zusya of Hanipol, "they will not ask me: 'Why were you not more like Moses our teacher?' They will ask me: 'Why were you not more like Zusya?'"[15]

The vision of the iris of Gilboa is forever in my heart. It has become a symbol, a reminder of the power of passion. I search for meaning and purpose, I search for work that is truly important, that will bring comfort and curiosity to people, that will deepen our connection to God and to one another, that will pull away the opaque veil that blocks out an internal light, the light within given by God at the moment of creation. This is my passion, and my *mitzvah* is the birthing of this passion into the world, it is the doing of all I can to live and breathe my mission. Every day that I grow, deepen, and spiritually mature, I come closer to the divine reason for my life.

What is your passion? Don't be afraid to ask. Do not be afraid to answer.

DIVINE DISCONTENT

Late at night there is an eerie glow seeping into my bedroom. The air is the color of transparent steel; there is a hard tint of gray silver. I have seen it, touched it, I have even stared it down. It doesn't help, though. The light talks to me, pulls at me, seeps into my lungs, making me itch from the inside out.

I don't like the glow, I don't understand it, but all attempts to rid myself of it seem in vain. After having breathed it in, it stays with me like ether, fogging my mind during the day. Always nagging, but not telling, not demanding; it is simply there like an internal ache. Even if I go to sleep completely exhausted for nights on end, there will come a night when I awake to see the gray glow hanging in the air like a cloud.

In the Book of Exodus, God is in the cloud.

What then is this late-night call all about? It is hard to understand a voice so distant and foreign; I seek only what I know. And yet that voice seems to call me to a different path. I crave comfort, not confusion. I seek knowing, not adventure. I yearn for the familiar, not new and untested ways of being. But there is more to my life than what I have come to expect.

Am I being called to leave the comfortable habit of my life? Have I been summoned to challenge the assumptions that make my life routine? Everything is fine, and yet I have this nagging sense that there should be more. That habit and routine somehow bar the way to rising to new levels of understanding and wonder.

Poet Leah Goldberg writes her prayer about the simplicity of life and yet asks God to "Teach my lips a blessing and a song of praise, To renew my day morning and night, Lest my day, today—like yesterday, Lest my day be merely routine."[16]

I am being called to rise out of the habit that has become my life.

Divine discontent is God's call to meaning. It begs us not to settle down before our time. Life is to be lived through us; through us can flow the gentle powers of the universe—the powers of healing, of kindness, of goodness.

Divine discontent is an internal restlessness, proving to us through the itch in our souls that there is more to life than we are living at the moment—that there are great things to do, that there is more to learn and understand.

Divine discontent is a hairline crack in our complacency.

My daughter Talia sits across from me writing a term paper on the historical themes of duty and obligation. She takes a break from Woodrow Wilson and Dalton Trumbo to look out the window in a dreamy pause. I ask, "Talia, do you know what divine discontent is?" She looks at me through her wire-rimmed glasses. "Let me see what you have written," she says. We switch seats. I begin reading about Wilson's call to service, and she reads what I have written about God's ambiguous call.

She then writes on my computer the following: "A voice beckons to me in the stillness. It is a voice that is foreign, distant. Is it my own or from somewhere else? It is only when I can align this Voice in harmony to my own that I may proceed down my path. I've felt the wind at my side and seen the clouds move in thunderous rage. I've heard the sweet song of a morning lark and known an indescribable love. Now I must..."

I interrupt her. We switch seats again. Back at my computer, I read what she has written. She has felt it too, I think to myself. That late-night call, that message in the wind. What must I do, how shall I respond?

I do believe in calling. Not only of priests, ministers, and rabbis. I believe that we all have been called to greatness, called to serve, called to bear witness to the beauty in the world, called to change our corner of it.

In the scrolls of our ancient text we read of calling. It all begins in the wilderness, a place beyond the boundaries of settlement, a place that is raw, wild, uninhibited, and unencumbered by our expectations of what should be. It is a place of possibility. This is God's country; it is a place where the horizon seems so distant, and the mountain so tall.

> Moses, tending the flock of his father-in-law, Jethro, the priest of Midian, drove the flock into the wilderness and came to Horeb, the mountain of God. An angel of God appeared to him in a blazing fire out of a bush. He gazed, and there was the bush all aflame, yet the bush was not consumed. Moses said, "I must look at this marvelous sight; why doesn't the bush burn up?" When God saw that he had turned to look, God called to him out of the bush, "Moses, Moses." He answered, "Here I am." "Do not come closer. Remove your sandals from your feet, for the place on which you stand is holy ground."[17]

All of Jewish theology can be summarized by this passage. God calls, and we are to answer *Heneni,* "Here I am." I am to be present in the Presence of God. I may not understand or even resist, but I hear that I have been summoned to pay attention to the world of the Spirit, and I am here.

But what follows is the uneasiness that comes from divine discontent. Moses is satisfied as a shepherd. He has married, found a home, and yet there is a call to service. He is reluctant to heed God's request. Three times he hesitates, saying that he is not fit for the task. Who will I say sent me to Egypt to free my people? What if they don't believe me? And finally: "Please God, I have never been a man of words, either in times past or now that you have

spoken to your servant; I am slow of speech and slow of tongue."
Moses has been called to persuade Pharaoh to let the Israelites go
free, and yet the skill he needs most, speech, he does not have.

God answers, "Who gives man speech? Who makes him dumb
or deaf, seeing or blind? Is it not I, God?" God says to Moses, I
know who you are and who you are not, I have made you what you
are with your abilities and disabilities, now answer the call.

Apparently doubt is part of it. Apparently perfection is not.

Divine discontent awakens me from my slumber, urges me
onward, insists that I be present in the presence of Divinity. That
makes my soul toss and turn until I cry out in the steel-colored
darkness, "Enough! I am here, now do with me what you will!"

MORTALITY DEMANDS

For Laurel Sorman z"l

I have faced mortality at age forty-three with the same force as I did on a summer day at the beach when I was three or so. It was rare for us to go to the beach, despite all my begging and my brother's pleading. My father did not like the sun burning his pale flesh. My mother did not like the sand scratching between her toes.

But this day we did go. Right after our sandy lunch, my father walked dutifully off to a shack in the distance to buy us ice cream. I squinted into the sunlight as I watched him walk off and decided to follow. I forgot to tell my mother that I was going. I walked and walked and walked, and the sand burned my feet so terribly that I can still feel the scorch on my soles.

I must have started to cry for my Daddy; he'd vanished into the horizon. I was hopelessly lost and scared, and my feet were ablaze. I did not know it, but as I cried for my father, my mother, discovering that I was gone, was madly running up and down the shore staring into the ocean, crying for me. I was lost, she thought, forever. My Daddy was lost, I thought, forever. I understood mortality in the panic and isolation we felt, invisible to one another among the sands.

Suddenly, a strong young lifeguard scooped me up in his arms. My feet were red from the burning sand, my cheeks were red from the burning tears as I sobbed into his suntan-lotioned body. He had found me, and then he found them, and all was well. But from time to time, we still tell the story.

About forty years later, I watched my father disappear into the sterile horizon of an operating room. He was not in search of ice cream but of a cleaner, more efficient blood flow to his heart. They called it a quadruple bypass, a surgery that has become as routine as root canal. I, his daughter, called it open-heart surgery, a brush with mortality. My mother and I tried to amuse each other during the hours it took to operate. But in our hearts we privately called out his name. I called for Daddy, she called for Norman, we both prayed that God did not call for his soul. There it was again, after all these years, the panic and isolation of the small child within me, previously invisible among the sands of time.

During the hours in the surgical waiting room and the days in the cardiac ward during his recovery, I saw hundreds of heart patients pass through. There were those who were recovering, those who were waiting, those who were scared, those who were relieved. There were those who were dying. Despite our many differences of size, age, color, and background, we had one thing in common: we became part of a club, privy to the secret that life is not forever. We were experiencing a crash that felt like the great salty ocean smacking us unaware in the face, when all we wanted to do was ride the waves.

It's enough to knock the breath out of you.

My friend who struggles with breast cancer says none of us makes it out of this life alive.

It is not unusual for us to deny our mortality. But it can't be spiritually sound to do so. Life is so damn short. That is not a cliché, it is the truth. It is possible that the awareness—not the fear, but the awareness—that our time is short could help us find perspective and balance. If death could come at any moment, then why would I spend this moment angry, resentful, and unforgiving?

Before Moses died, the legend tells us, he fought and fought against his mortality, trying to bargain, trick, and deceive the

Angel of Death. Finally God intervened. God took away his soul with a kiss. The legend ends, "and God wept."

At this moment, with the hospital smell still on my clothes, I feel Moses' struggle. I feel his struggle to live grounded in this world while needing to ascend the highest mountain the spirit will allow. I feel his yearning to travel yet one more journey, to cross one more river. I feel his passion to live deeply, truly, and forever.

I can't help but wonder why it is so hard to live the words I write. I believe them, I teach them, I write them to you, and I know that one of the hardest acts of the human spirit is forgiveness. But at this moment, with the image of my father in the recovery room seared into my brain—moments after surgery, helplessly dead to the world, with tubes coming and going from his frail body—I can't help but wonder: How do I keep the fact of mortality from driving me insane? How do I use mortality as a gift to teach me to live my life more fully and with less pettiness? I want to learn to live in the light of God's goodness and not in the darkness of human frailty. I reject the notion and reality of lingering hurt. I want to be forgiven. Therefore I must forgive.

It is odd, don't you think, that it seems easier for us to hate than to love, to hold on rather than to let go.

This I know: I want my soul to be taken like that of Moses...with a kiss. I want God to weep when I bury my parents, may they live a hundred and twenty years. And in the meantime, I want to live as a trusting child as often as I can, playing on the beach, protected from true danger.

As a person enters the world, so he departs.
He enters the world with a cry, and he departs with a cry.
He enters the world weeping and leaves it weeping.
He enters the world with love, and leaves it with love.
He enters the world with a sigh, and leaves it with a sigh.
He enters the world devoid of knowledge, and leaves it devoid of knowledge.

It has been taught in the name of Rabbi Meir:

> When a person enters the world his hands are clenched as though to say, "The whole world is mine. I shall inherit it."
>
> But when he leaves, his hands are spread open as though to say, "I have taken nothing from the world."[18]

The gift of our lives remains constant from the moment we are born to the moment we die.

We love, cry, sigh, and weep from birth to death. And the truth about the vastness of the spiritual and physical worlds is that it is ultimately unknowable from the day we are born until the day we die. If this is indeed the way of the world, it should bring us comfort. Life is a blessing. All of it. And though in our youth we are hungry and impatient, grasping and clutching the pain, the love, the varied experiences, the possibility that we will understand, as we age we learn to let go, unclench the fist, thus living a bit more gently. There isn't a life that is lived without tears and disappointments. The goal is not to eliminate the pain but to learn from it, to grow and expand because of it.

Perhaps the opposite of forgiveness is holding on. Holding on to anger and resentment. Holding on to offense and indignation. Holding on to a sense that somehow life is to be lived without conflict. Life *is* conflict. Witness the Colorado River raging against the canyon, and you see conflict and danger and beauty and inspiration all in one. Do we attempt to obliterate the river, or learn to respect its complexity?

We come into this world with a fist; how do we learn to leave with our hand open and extended? Can't we spend our days learning to let go? To forgive is to yield to the complexity of life, to its richness. To forgive is to allow ourselves to release our grasp on hurt and open our hearts to love.

Lost on the sands over forty years ago, I had my first lesson in mortality. It scared me; I felt exposed and unsafe. But today I feel compelled by mortality to live with joy, allowing life's experiences be as the high tides and low tides, washing away and revealing all of life's treasures as endless waves of beauty.

Enlightenment rises like the dawn at the edge of my life. I seek the secret code. The Dance of the Dolphin, as it gracefully navigates water and air, tells me to find a balance because life is a mystery of contradictions, worlds I know and those I don't, realities I can see and those that I can only sense. We live with paradox and ambiguity. We live in our minds and in our souls. We live in our own world and in the world of all. And all the while we dance, sometimes with grace, and sometimes not.

Dear God, teach me the steps, synchronize my heart with the rhythms of your Truth, take my hand and lead.

NOTES

Prayer: The Language of the Spirit

1. Sylvia Plath, "Stillborn," in *Crossing the Water* (New York: Harper & Row, 1971), p. 20.
2. Meyer Levin, *Classic Hassidic Tales* (New York: Dorset, 1985), pp. 132–134.
3. Meyer Levin, *Classic Hassidic Tales* (New York: Dorset, 1985), pp. 132–137.
4. *Gates of Prayer* (New York: Central Conference of American Rabbis, 1975), p. 92.
5. Anne Lamott, *Traveling Mercies: Some Thoughts on Faith* (New York: Anchor Books, 2000), p. 82.
6. Laurie Beth Jones, *The Path* (New York: Hyperion, 1996), p. 23.
7. Ellen Frankel, *The Classic Tales: 4000 Years of Jewish Lore* (New York: Jason Aronson, 1989), p. 557.
8. Annie Dillard, *For the Time Being* (New York: Knopf, 1999), p. 89.
9. BT *Hagiga* 14b.
10. Adapted from Arthur Green and Barry W. Holtz, eds., *Your Word Is Fire: The Hasidic Masters on Contemplative Prayer* (Woodstock, Vt.: Jewish Lights, 1993).
11. Martin Buber, *I and Thou* (New York: Scribner's, 1958), p. 137.
12. Exodus 33:7.
13. This story begins with the Book of Numbers, chapter 22.

14. Rainer Maria Rilke, "Just as the Winged Energy of Delight," in *Selected Poems*, trans. Robert Bly (New York: Harper & Row, 1981), p. 175.
15. Compiled from various High Holiday prayer books.
16. BT *Brachot* 17.
17. Psalm 19.
18. Janet Fitch, *White Oleander* (Boston: Little, Brown, 1999).

Perspective: The Language of Thought

1. BT *Shabbat* 119b.
2. Marion Woodman, *Bone* (New York: Viking, 2000), p. xvi.
3. BT *Shabbat* 31a.
4. Anne Cameron, *Daughters of Copper Woman* (Vancouver, B.C.: Press Gang Publishing, 1981), pp. 44–46.
5. Martin Buber, *Martin Buber's Ten Rungs* (New York: Carol Publishing, 1995), p. 79.
6. Annie Dillard, *Pilgrim at Tinker Creek* (New York: HarperCollins, 1974), p. 33.
7. BT *Berachot* 58.
8. From the evening liturgy, *Hashkevenu* prayer.
9. Dava Sobel, *Galileo's Daughter* (New York: Walker, 1999), p. 12.
10. Viktor Frankl, *Man's Search for Meaning* (New York: Simon & Schuster, 1984), pp. 77–78.
11. Ralph Waldo Emerson, *Self-Reliance* (New York: Peter Pauper, 1967), p. 21.
12. James Hillman, *The Soul's Code: In Search of Character and Calling* (New York: Warner, 1996), pp. 5–7.

Meaning

1. Adapted from Arthur Green and Barry W. Holtz, eds., *Your Word Is Fire: The Hasidic Masters on Contemplative Prayer* (Woodstock, Vt.: Jewish Lights, 1993), pp. 109–110.
2. *Pirke Avot* 2:5.

3. Gregg Levoy, *Callings: Finding and Following an Authentic Life* (New York: Harmony, 1997), p. 49.

4. Chick Corea, *Return to Forever* (ECM, 1972).

5. Christina Rossetti, "Who Can See the Wind" (1872).

6. Genesis 33:25–30.

7. See "Vayera," in *The Women's Torah Commentary: New Insights from Women Rabbis on the 54 Weekly Torah Portions*, ed. by Rabbi Elyse Goldstein (Woodstock, Vt.: Jewish Lights, 2000).

8. Frankel, *Classic Tales*.

9. Mary Caroline Richards, "Centering," in *Cries of the Spirit*, ed. Marilyn Sewell (Boston: Beacon, 1991), p. 58.

10. *Bereshit Rabbah* 5:4.

11. BT *Hagigah* 12a.

12. Adapted from Frankel, *Classic Tales*, pp. 557–560.

13. Yehuda Amichai, *Open Closed Open* (New York: Harcourt, 2000), p. 41.

14. Thank you to Rabbi Michael Balinsky of the Florence Melton Adult Mini School for sharing these two passages, from Rabbi Mordechai Joseph Leiner of Izbica and *Midrash Tehillim*, with me.

15. Frankel, *Classic Tales*, p. 516.

16. Goldberg, Leah, *Prayerbook Avodah Sheblov* (Jerusalem: The Israel Movement for Progressive Judasim, 1981). Translation is mine.

17. Exodus 3:1–5.

18. *Ecclesiates Rabbah*, chapter 5. The legend of Moses and this midrash came together for me when I read Francine Klagsbrun, *Voices of Wisdom: Jewish Ideals and Ethics for Everyday Living* (New York: Jonathon David, 1980).

About JEWISH LIGHTS Publishing

People of all faiths and backgrounds yearn for books that attract, engage, educate and spiritually inspire.

Our principal goal is to stimulate thought and help all people learn about who the Jewish People are, where they come from, and what the future can be made to hold. While people of our diverse Jewish heritage are the primary audience, our books speak to people in the Christian world as well and will broaden their understanding of Judaism and the roots of their own faith.

We bring to you authors who are at the forefront of spiritual thought and experience. While each has something different to say, they all say it in a voice that you can hear.

Our books are designed to welcome you and then to engage, stimulate and inspire. We judge our success not only by whether or not our books are beautiful and commercially successful, but by whether or not they make a difference in your life.

We at Jewish Lights take great care to produce beautiful books that present meaningful spiritual content in a form that reflects the art of making high quality books. Therefore, we want to acknowledge those who contributed to the production of this book.

Stuart M. Matlins, Publisher

PRODUCTION
Tim Holtz & Bridgett Taylor

EDITORIAL
Amanda Dupuis, Martha McKinney,
Polly Short Mahoney & Emily Wichland

JACKET DESIGN & TYPESETTING
Drena Fagen, New York, New York

INTERIOR DESIGN
Susan Ramundo, SR Desktop Services, Ridge, New York

INTERIOR TYPESETTING
Reuben Kantor, QEP Design, Jamaica Plain, Massachusetts

JACKET / TEXT PRINTING & BINDING
Lake Book, Melrose Park, Illinois

The Way Into... Series

A major 14-volume series to be completed over the next several years, **The Way Into...** provides an accessible and usable "guided tour" of the Jewish faith, its people, its history and beliefs—in total, an introduction to Judaism for adults that will enable them to understand and interact with sacred texts. Each volume is written by a major modern scholar and teacher, and is organized around an important concept of Judaism.

The Way Into... will enable all readers to achieve a real sense of Jewish cultural literacy through guided study. Available volumes include:

  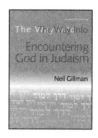 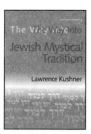

The Way Into Torah

by *Dr. Norman J. Cohen*

What is "Torah"? What are the different approaches to studying Torah? What are the different levels of understanding Torah? For whom is the study intended? Explores the origins and development of Torah, why it should be studied and how to do it.

6 x 9, 176 pp, HC, ISBN 1-58023-028-8 **$21.95**

The Way Into Jewish Prayer

by *Dr. Lawrence A. Hoffman*

Opens the door to 3,000 years of the Jewish way to God by making available all you need to feel at home in Jewish worship. Provides basic definitions of the terms you need to know as well as thoughtful analysis of the depth that lies beneath Jewish prayer.

6 x 9, 224 pp, HC, ISBN 1-58023-027-X **$21.95**

The Way Into Encountering God in Judaism

by *Dr. Neil Gillman*

Explains how Jews have encountered God throughout history—and today—by exploring the many metaphors for God in Jewish tradition. Explores the Jewish tradition's passionate but also conflicting ways of relating to God as Creator, relational partner, and a force in history and nature.

6 x 9, 240 pp, HC, ISBN 1-58023-025-3 **$21.95**

The Way Into Jewish Mystical Tradition

by *Rabbi Lawrence Kushner*

Explains the principles of Jewish mystical thinking, their religious and spiritual significance, and how they relate to our lives. A book that allows us to experience and understand the Jewish mystical approach to our place in the world.

6 x 9, 224 pp, HC, ISBN 1-58023-029-6 **$21.95**

Or phone, fax, mail or e-mail to: **JEWISH LIGHTS** Publishing

Sunset Farm Offices, Route 4 • P.O. Box 237 • Woodstock, Vermont 05091

Tel: (802) 457-4000 • Fax: (802) 457-4004 • www.jewishlights.com

Credit card orders: (800) 962-4544 (9AM–5PM ET Monday–Friday)

Generous discounts on quantity orders. SATISFACTION GUARANTEED. Prices subject to change.

Spirituality

My People's Prayer Book: *Traditional Prayers, Modern Commentaries*
Ed. by *Dr. Lawrence A. Hoffman*

Provides a diverse and exciting commentary to the traditional liturgy, helping modern men and women find new wisdom in Jewish prayer, and bring liturgy into their lives. Each book includes Hebrew text, modern translation, and commentaries *from all perspectives* of the Jewish world.

Vol. 1—*The Sh'ma and Its Blessings,* 7 x 10, 168 pp, HC, ISBN 1-879045-79-6 **$23.95**
Vol. 2—*The Amidah,* 7 x 10, 240 pp, HC, ISBN 1-879045-80-X **$23.95**
Vol. 3—*P'sukei D'zimrah* (Morning Psalms), 7 x 10, 240 pp, HC, ISBN 1-879045-81-8 **$24.95**
Vol. 4—*Seder K'riat Hatorah* (The Torah Service), 7 x 10, 264 pp, ISBN 1-879045-82-6 **$23.95**
Vol. 5—*Birkhot Hashachar* (Morning Blessings), 7 x 10, 256 pp, ISBN 1-879045-83-4 **$24.95**

(Vol. 5 avail. Fall 2001)

   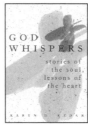 

Becoming a Congregation of Learners
Learning as a Key to Revitalizing Congregational Life by Isa Aron, Ph.D.;
Foreword by Rabbi Lawrence A. Hoffman, Co-Developer, Synagogue 2000
6 x 9, 304 pp, Quality PB, ISBN 1-58023-089-X **$19.95**

Self, Struggle & Change
Family Conflict Stories in Genesis and Their Healing Insights for Our Lives
by Dr. Norman J. Cohen 6 x 9, 224 pp, Quality PB, ISBN 1-879045-66-4 **$16.95**;
HC, ISBN 1-879045-19-2 **$21.95**

Voices from Genesis: *Guiding Us through the Stages of Life*
by Dr. Norman J. Cohen 6 x 9, 192 pp, Quality PB, ISBN 1-58023-118-7 **$16.95**;
HC, ISBN 1-879045-75-3 **$21.95**

God Whispers: *Stories of the Soul, Lessons of the Heart*
by Rabbi Karyn D. Kedar 6 x 9, 176 pp, Quality PB, ISBN 1-58023-088-1 **$15.95**

The Business Bible: *10 New Commandments for Bringing Spirituality & Ethical Values into the Workplace*
by Rabbi Wayne Dosick 5½ x 8½, 208 pp, Quality PB, ISBN 1-58023-101-2 **$14.95**

Being God's Partner: *How to Find the Hidden Link Between Spirituality and Your Work*
by Rabbi Jeffrey K. Salkin; Intro. by Norman Lear AWARD WINNER!
6 x 9, 192 pp, Quality PB, ISBN 1-879045-65-6 **$16.95**; HC, ISBN 1-879045-37-0 **$19.95**

God & the Big Bang
Discovering Harmony Between Science & Spirituality AWARD WINNER!
by Daniel C. Matt 6 x 9, 224 pp, Quality PB, ISBN 1-879045-89-3 **$16.95**

Soul Judaism: *Dancing with God into a New Era*
by Rabbi Wayne Dosick 5½ x 8½, 304 pp, Quality PB, ISBN 1-58023-053-9 **$16.95**

Finding Joy: *A Practical Spiritual Guide to Happiness* AWARD WINNER!
by Rabbi Dannel I. Schwartz with Mark Hass
6 x 9, 192 pp, Quality PB, ISBN 1-58023-009-1 **$14.95**; HC, ISBN 1-879045-53-2 **$19.95**

Theology/Philosophy

Love and Terror in the God Encounter: *The Theological Legacy of Rabbi Joseph B. Soloveitchik, Vol. 1* by *Dr. David Hartman*

Renowned scholar David Hartman explores the sometimes surprising intersection of Soloveitchik's rootedness in halakhic tradition with his genuine responsiveness to modern Western theology. An engaging look at one of the most important Jewish thinkers of the twentieth century. 6 x 9, 240 pp, HC, ISBN 1-58023-112-8 **$25.00**

These Are the Words: *A Vocabulary of Jewish Spiritual Life*

by *Arthur Green*

What are the most essential ideas, concepts and terms that an educated person needs to know about Judaism? From *Adonai* (My Lord) to *zekhut* (merit), this enlightening and entertaining journey through Judaism teaches us the 149 core Hebrew words that constitute the basic vocabulary of Jewish spiritual life. 6 x 9, 304 pp, Quality PB, ISBN 1-58023-107-1 **$18.95**

Broken Tablets: *Restoring the Ten Commandments and Ourselves*

Ed. by *Rabbi Rachel S. Mikva*; Intro. by *Rabbi Lawrence Kushner* AWARD WINNER!

Twelve outstanding spiritual leaders each share profound and personal thoughts about these biblical commands and why they have such a special hold on us.
6 x 9, 192 pp, HC, ISBN 1-58023-066-0 **$21.95**

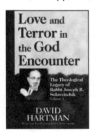  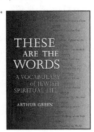 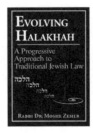 

A Heart of Many Rooms: *Celebrating the Many Voices within Judaism* AWARD WINNER!
by Dr. David Hartman 6 x 9, 352 pp, HC, ISBN 1-58023-048-2 **$24.95**

A Living Covenant: *The Innovative Spirit in Traditional Judaism* AWARD WINNER!
by Dr. David Hartman 6 x 9, 368 pp, Quality PB, ISBN 1-58023-011-3 **$18.95**

Evolving Halakhah: *A Progressive Approach to Traditional Jewish Law*
by Rabbi Dr. Moshe Zemer 6 x 9, 480 pp, HC, ISBN 1-58023-002-4 **$40.00**

The Death of Death: *Resurrection and Immortality in Jewish Thought* AWARD WINNER!
by Dr. Neil Gillman 6 x 9, 336 pp, Quality PB, ISBN 1-58023-081-4 **$18.95**

The Last Trial: *On the Legends and Lore of the Command to Abraham to Offer Isaac as a Sacrifice* by Shalom Spiegel 6 x 9, 208 pp, Quality PB, ISBN 1-879045-29-X **$17.95**

Tormented Master: *The Life and Spiritual Quest of Rabbi Nahman of Bratslav*
by Dr. Arthur Green 6 x 9, 416 pp, Quality PB, ISBN 1-879045-11-7 **$18.95**

The Earth Is the Lord's: *The Inner World of the Jew in Eastern Europe*
by Abraham Joshua Heschel 5½ x 8, 128 pp, Quality PB, ISBN 1-879045-42-7 **$14.95**

A Passion for Truth: *Despair and Hope in Hasidism* by Abraham Joshua Heschel
5½ x 8, 352 pp, Quality PB, ISBN 1-879045-41-9 **$18.95**

Your Word Is Fire: *The Hasidic Masters on Contemplative Prayer* Ed. by Dr. Arthur Green and Dr. Barry W. Holtz 6 x 9, 160 pp, Quality PB, ISBN 1-879045-25-7 **$14.95**

Life Cycle/Grief

Against the Dying of the Light
A Parent's Story of Love, Loss and Hope
by *Leonard Fein*

The sudden death of a child. A personal tragedy beyond description. Rage and despair deeper than sorrow. What can come from it? Raw wisdom and defiant hope. In this unusual exploration of heartbreak and healing, Fein chronicles the sudden death of his 30-year-old daughter and reveals what the progression of grief can teach each one of us.
5½ x 8½, 176 pp, HC, ISBN 1-58023-110-1 **$19.95**

Mourning & Mitzvah, 2nd Ed.: *A Guided Journal for Walking the Mourner's Path through Grief to Healing* with *Over 60 Guided Exercises*
by *Anne Brener, L.C.S.W.*

For those who mourn a death, for those who would help them, for those who face a loss of any kind, Brener teaches us the power and strength available to us in the fully experienced mourning process. Revised and expanded. 7½ x 9, 304 pp, Quality PB, ISBN 1-58023-113-6 **$19.95**

Grief in Our Seasons: *A Mourner's Kaddish Companion*
by *Rabbi Kerry M. Olitzky*

A wise and inspiring selection of sacred Jewish writings and a simple, powerful ancient ritual for mourners to read each day, to help hold the memory of their loved ones in their hearts. Offers a comforting, step-by-step daily link to saying Kaddish.
4½ x 6½, 448 pp, Quality PB, ISBN 1-879045-55-9 **$15.95**

   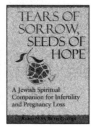 

Tears of Sorrow, Seeds of Hope
A Jewish Spiritual Companion for Infertility and Pregnancy Loss
by Rabbi Nina Beth Cardin   6 x 9, 192 pp, HC, ISBN 1-58023-017-2 **$19.95**

A Time to Mourn, A Time to Comfort
A Guide to Jewish Bereavement and Comfort
by Dr. Ron Wolfson   7 x 9, 336 pp, Quality PB, ISBN 1-879045-96-6 **$18.95**

When a Grandparent Dies
A Kid's Own Remembering Workbook for Dealing with Shiva and the Year Beyond
by Nechama Liss-Levinson, Ph.D.
8 x 10, 48 pp, HC, Illus., 2-color text, ISBN 1-879045-44-3 **$15.95**

Healing/Wellness/Recovery

Jewish Paths toward Healing and Wholeness
A Personal Guide to Dealing with Suffering
by *Rabbi Kerry M. Olitzky*; Foreword by *Debbie Friedman*

Why me? Why do we suffer? How can we heal? Grounded in personal experience with illness and Jewish spiritual traditions, this book provides healing rituals, psalms and prayers that help readers initiate a dialogue with God, to guide them along the complicated path of healing and wholeness. 6 x 9, 192 pp, Quality PB, ISBN 1-58023-068-7 **$15.95**

Healing of Soul, Healing of Body
Spiritual Leaders Unfold the Strength & Solace in Psalms
Ed. by *Rabbi Simkha Y. Weintraub, CSW,* for The National Center for Jewish Healing

A source of solace for those who are facing illness, as well as those who care for them. Provides a wellspring of strength with inspiring introductions and commentaries by eminent spiritual leaders reflecting all Jewish movements.
6 x 9, 128 pp, Quality PB, Illus., 2-color text, ISBN 1-879045-31-1 **$14.95**

Jewish Pastoral Care
A Practical Handbook from Traditional and Contemporary Sources
Ed. by *Rabbi Dayle A. Friedman*

Gives today's Jewish pastoral counselors practical guidelines based in the Jewish tradition.
6 x 9, 464 pp, HC, ISBN 1-58023-078-4 **$35.00**

Twelve Jewish Steps to Recovery: *A Personal Guide to Turning from Alcoholism & Other Addictions . . . Drugs, Food, Gambling, Sex . . .* by Rabbi Kerry M. Olitzky & Stuart A. Copans, M.D. Preface by Abraham J. Twerski, M.D.; Intro. by Rabbi Sheldon Zimmerman; "Getting Help" by JACS Foundation 6 x 9, 144 pp, Quality PB, ISBN 1-879045-09-5 **$13.95**

One Hundred Blessings Every Day: *Daily Twelve Step Recovery Affirmations, Exercises for Personal Growth & Renewal Reflecting Seasons of the Jewish Year* by Rabbi Kerry M. Olitzky 4½ x 6½, 432 pp, Quality PB, ISBN 1-879045-30-3 **$14.95**

Recovery from Codependence: *A Jewish Twelve Steps Guide to Healing Your Soul* by Rabbi Kerry M. Olitzky 6 x 9, 160 pp, Quality PB, ISBN 1-879045-32-X **$13.95**; HC, ISBN 1-879045-27-3 **$21.95**

Renewed Each Day: *Daily Twelve Step Recovery Meditations Based on the Bible* by Rabbi Kerry M. Olitzky & Aaron Z. *Vol. I: Genesis & Exodus*; *Vol. II: Leviticus, Numbers and Deuteronomy*
Vol. I: 6 x 9, 224 pp, Quality PB, ISBN 1-879045-12-5 **$14.95**
Vol. II: 6 x 9, 280 pp, Quality PB, ISBN 1-879045-13-3 **$14.95**

Life Cycle & Holidays

How to Be a Perfect Stranger, 2nd Ed. In 2 Volumes
A Guide to Etiquette in Other People's Religious Ceremonies
Ed. by *Stuart M. Matlins* & *Arthur J. Magida* **AWARD WINNER!**

What will happen? What do I do? What do I wear? What do I say? What are their basic beliefs? Should I bring a gift? Explains the rituals and celebrations of North America's major religions/denominations, helping an interested guest to feel comfortable. *Not* presented from the perspective of any particular faith. SKYLIGHT PATHS Books
Vol. 1: *North America's Largest Faiths*, 6 x 9, 432 pp, Quality PB, ISBN 1-893361-01-2 **$19.95**
Vol. 2: *Other Faiths in North America*, 6 x 9, 416 pp, Quality PB, ISBN 1-893361-02-0 **$19.95**

Celebrating Your New Jewish Daughter
Creating Jewish Ways to Welcome Baby Girls into the Covenant— New and Traditional Ceremonies
by *Debra Nussbaum Cohen*; Foreword by *Rabbi Sandy Eisenberg Sasso*

Features everything families need to plan a celebration that reflects Jewish tradition, including a how-to guide to new and traditional ceremonies, and practical guidelines for planning the joyous event. 6 x 9, 272 pp, Quality PB, ISBN 1-58023-090-3 **$18.95**

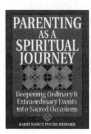    

The New Jewish Baby Book **AWARD WINNER!**
Names, Ceremonies & Customs—A Guide for Today's Families
by Anita Diamant 6 x 9, 336 pp, Quality PB, ISBN 1-879045-28-1 **$18.95**

Parenting As a Spiritual Journey
Deepening Ordinary & Extraordinary Events into Sacred Occasions
by Rabbi Nancy Fuchs-Kreimer 6 x 9, 224 pp, Quality PB, ISBN 1-58023-016-4 **$16.95**

Putting God on the Guest List, 2nd Ed. **AWARD WINNER!**
How to Reclaim the Spiritual Meaning of Your Child's Bar or Bat Mitzvah
by Rabbi Jeffrey K. Salkin 6 x 9, 224 pp, Quality PB, ISBN 1-879045-59-1 **$16.95**

For Kids—Putting God on Your Guest List
How to Claim the Spiritual Meaning of Your Bar or Bat Mitzvah
by Rabbi Jeffrey K. Salkin 6 x 9, 144 pp, Quality PB, ISBN 1-58023-015-6 **$14.95**

Bar/Bat Mitzvah Basics, 2nd Ed.: *A Practical Family Guide to Coming of Age Together*
Ed. by Cantor Helen Leneman 6 x 9, 240 pp, Quality PB, ISBN 1-58023-151-9 **$18.95**

Hanukkah: The Art of Jewish Living
by Dr. Ron Wolfson 7 x 9, 192 pp, Quality PB, Illus., ISBN 1-879045-97-4 **$16.95**

The Shabbat Seder: The Art of Jewish Living
by Dr. Ron Wolfson 7 x 9, 272 pp, Quality PB, Illus., ISBN 1-879045-90-7 **$16.95**

The Passover Seder: The Art of Jewish Living
by Dr. Ron Wolfson 7 x 9, 352 pp, Quality PB, Illus., ISBN 1-879045-93-1 **$16.95**

Children's Spirituality

ENDORSED BY CATHOLIC, PROTESTANT, AND JEWISH RELIGIOUS LEADERS
MULTICULTURAL, NONDENOMINATIONAL, NONSECTARIAN

God Said Amen

For ages 4 & up

by *Sandy Eisenberg Sasso*
Full-color illus. by *Avi Katz*

A warm and inspiring tale of two kingdoms: one overflowing with water but without oil to light its lamps; the other blessed with oil but no water to grow its gardens. The kingdoms' rulers ask God for help but are too stubborn to ask each other. It takes a minstrel, a pair of royal riding-birds and their young keepers, and a simple act of kindness to show that they need only reach out to each other to find God's answer to their prayers.

9 x 12, 32 pp, HC, Full-color illus., ISBN 1-58023-080-6 **$16.95**

For Heaven's Sake

For ages 4 & up

by *Sandy Eisenberg Sasso*; Full-color illus. by *Kathryn Kunz Finney*

Everyone talked about heaven: "Thank heavens." "Heaven forbid." "For heaven's sake, Isaiah." But no one would say what heaven was or how to find it. So Isaiah decides to find out, by seeking answers from many different people.
9 x 12, 32 pp, HC, Full-color illus., ISBN 1-58023-054-7 **$16.95**

But God Remembered

For ages 8 & up

Stories of Women from Creation to the Promised Land

by *Sandy Eisenberg Sasso*; Full-color illus. by *Bethanne Andersen*

A fascinating collection of four different stories of women only briefly mentioned in biblical tradition and religious texts. Vibrantly brings to life courageous and strong women from ancient tradition; all teach important values through their actions and faith.
9 x 12, 32 pp, HC, Full-color illus., ISBN 1-879045-43-5 **$16.95**

God in Between

For ages 4 & up

by *Sandy Eisenberg Sasso*; Full-color illus. by *Sally Sweetland*

If you wanted to find God, where would you look? A magical, mythical tale that teaches that God can be found where we are: within all of us and the relationships between us.
9 x 12, 32 pp, HC, Full-color illus., ISBN 1-879045-86-9 **$16.95**

For ages 4 & up

A Prayer for the Earth: The Story of Naamah, Noah's Wife

by *Sandy Eisenberg Sasso*; Full-color illus. by *Bethanne Andersen*

This new story, based on an ancient text, opens readers' religious imaginations to new ideas about the well-known story of the Flood. When God tells Noah to bring the animals of the world onto the ark, God also calls on Naamah, Noah's wife, to save each plant on Earth.
9 x 12, 32 pp, HC, Full-color illus., ISBN 1-879045-60-5 **$16.95**

Children's Spirituality

In Our Image
God's First Creatures
by *Nancy Sohn Swartz*
Full-color illus. by *Melanie Hall*

For ages 4 & up

A playful new twist on the Creation story—from the perspective of the animals. Celebrates the interconnectedness of nature and the harmony of all living things. "The vibrantly colored illustrations nearly leap off the page in this delightful interpretation." —*School Library Journal*

9 x 12, 32 pp, HC, Full-color illus., ISBN 1-879045-99-0 **$16.95**

 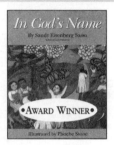 

God's Paintbrush

For ages 4 & up

by *Sandy Eisenberg Sasso*; Full-color illus. by *Annette Compton*

Invites children of all faiths and backgrounds to encounter God openly in their own lives. Wonderfully interactive; provides questions adult and child can explore together at the end of each episode.
11 x 8½, 32 pp, HC, Full-color illus., ISBN 1-879045-22-2 **$16.95**

Also available: A Teacher's Guide: **A Guide for Jewish & Christian Educators and Parents**
8½ x 11, 32 pp, PB, ISBN 1-879045-57-5 **$8.95**

God's Paintbrush Celebration Kit 9½ x 12, HC, Includes 5 sessions/40 full-color Activity Sheets and Teacher Folder with complete instructions, ISBN 1-58023-050-4 **$21.95**

In God's Name

For ages 4 & up

by *Sandy Eisenberg Sasso*; Full-color illus. by *Phoebe Stone*

Like an ancient myth in its poetic text and vibrant illustrations, this award-winning modern fable about the search for God's name celebrates the diversity and, at the same time, the unity of all the people of the world.
9 x 12, 32 pp, HC, Full-color illus., ISBN 1-879045-26-5 **$16.95**

What Is God's Name? (A Board Book)

For ages 0–4

An abridged board book version of the award-winning *In God's Name*.
5 x 5, 24 pp, Board, Full-color illus., ISBN 1-893361-10-1 **$7.95** A SKYLIGHT PATHS Book

The 11th Commandment: Wisdom from Our Children

For all ages

by *The Children of America*

"If there were an Eleventh Commandment, what would it be?" Children of many religious denominations across America answer this question—in their own drawings and words. "A rare book of spiritual celebration for all people, of all ages, for all time."—*Bookviews*
8 x 10, 48 pp, HC, Full-color illus., ISBN 1-879045-46-X **$16.95**

Children's Spirituality

Because Nothing Looks Like God

by *Lawrence and Karen Kushner*
Full-color illus. by *Dawn W. Majewski*

For ages 4 & up

MULTICULTURAL, NONDENOMINATIONAL, NONSECTARIAN

What is God like? The first collaborative work by husband-and-wife team Lawrence and Karen Kushner introduces children to the possibilities of spiritual life. Real-life examples of happiness and sadness—from goodnight stories, to the hope and fear felt the first time at bat, to the closing moments of life—invite us to explore, together with our children, the questions we all have about God, no matter what our age.

11 x 8½, 32 pp, HC, Full-color illus., ISBN 1-58023-092-X **$16.95**

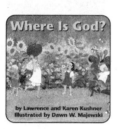

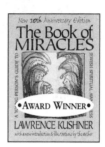

Where Is God?
What Does God Look Like?
How Does God Make Things Happen? (Board Books)

For ages 0–4

by *Lawrence and Karen Kushner*; Full-color illus. by *Dawn W. Majewski*

Gently invites children to become aware of God's presence all around them. Three board books abridged from *Because Nothing Looks Like God* by Lawrence and Karen Kushner.
Each 5 x 5, 24 pp, Board, Full-color illus. **$7.95**   SKYLIGHT PATHS Books

Sharing Blessings

Children's Stories for Exploring the Spirit of the Jewish Holidays
by *Rahel Musleah* and *Rabbi Michael Klayman*
Full-color illus. by *Mary O'Keefe Young*

For ages 6 & up

What is the spiritual message of each of the Jewish holidays? How do we teach it to our children? Many books tell children about the historical significance and customs of the holidays. Through stories about one family's preparation, *Sharing Blessings* explores ways to get into the *spirit* of 13 different holidays.
8½ x 11, 64 pp, HC, Full-color illus., ISBN 1-879045-71-0 **$18.95**

The Book of Miracles

A Young Person's Guide to Jewish Spiritual Awareness
by *Lawrence Kushner*

For ages 9 & up

Introduces kids to a way of everyday spiritual thinking to last a lifetime. Kushner, whose award-winning books have brought spirituality to life for countless adults, now shows young people how to use Judaism as a foundation on which to build their lives.
6 x 9, 96 pp, HC, 2-color illus., ISBN 1-879045-78-8 **$16.95**

Spirituality/Jewish Meditation

Discovering Jewish Meditation
Instruction & Guidance for Learning an Ancient Spiritual Practice
by *Nan Fink Gefen*

Gives readers of any level of understanding the tools to learn the practice of Jewish meditation on your own, starting you on the path to a deep spiritual and personal connection to God and to greater insight about your life. 6 x 9, 208 pp, Quality PB, ISBN 1-58023-067-9 **$16.95**

Entering the Temple of Dreams: *Jewish Prayers, Movements, and Meditations for the End of the Day* by *Tamar Frankiel* and *Judy Greenfeld*

Nighttime spirituality is much more than bedtime prayers! Here, you'll uncover deeper meaning to familiar nighttime prayers—and learn to combine the prayers with movements and meditations to enhance your physical and psychological well-being.
7 x 10, 192 pp, Quality PB, Illus., ISBN 1-58023-079-2 **$16.95**

One God Clapping: *The Spiritual Path of a Zen Rabbi* AWARD WINNER!
by *Alan Lew* with *Sherril Jaffe*

A fascinating personal story of a Jewish meditation expert's roundabout spiritual journey from Zen Buddhist practitioner to rabbi. 5½ x 8½, 336 pp, Quality PB, ISBN 1-58023-115-2 **$16.95**

 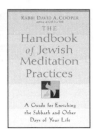   

The Handbook of Jewish Meditation Practices
A Guide for Enriching the Sabbath and Other Days of Your Life
by *Rabbi David A. Cooper*

Gives us ancient and modern Jewish tools—Jewish practices and traditions, easy-to-use meditation exercises, and contemplative study of Jewish sacred texts. 6 x 9, 208 pp, Quality PB, ISBN 1-58023-102-0 **$16.95**

Stepping Stones to Jewish Spiritual Living: *Walking the Path Morning, Noon, and Night*
by Rabbi James L. Mirel & Karen Bonnell Werth
6 x 9, 240 pp, Quality PB, ISBN 1-58023-074-1 **$16.95**

Meditation from the Heart of Judaism
Today's Teachers Share Their Practices, Techniques, and Faith
Ed. by Avram Davis 6 x 9, 256 pp, Quality PB, ISBN 1-58023-049-0 **$16.95**;
HC, ISBN 1-879045-77-X **$21.95**

The Way of Flame: *A Guide to the Forgotten Mystical Tradition of Jewish Meditation*
by Avram Davis 4½ x 8, 176 pp, Quality PB, ISBN 1-58023-060-1 **$15.95**

Minding the Temple of the Soul: *Balancing Body, Mind, and Spirit through Traditional Jewish Prayer, Movement, and Meditation*
by Tamar Frankiel and Judy Greenfeld 7 x 10, 184 pp, Quality PB, Illus.,
ISBN 1-879045-64-8 **$16.95**; Audiotape of the Blessings and Meditations (60-min. cassette), JN01
$9.95; Videotape of the Movements and Meditations (46-min.), S507 **$20.00**

Spirituality—The Kushner Series
Books by Lawrence Kushner

The Way Into Jewish Mystical Tradition

Explains the principles of Jewish mystical thinking, their religious and spiritual significance, and how they relate to our lives. A book that allows us to experience and understand the Jewish mystical approach to our place in the world. 6 x 9, 224 pp, HC, ISBN 1-58023-029-6 **$21.95**

Eyes Remade for Wonder
The Way of Jewish Mysticism and Sacred Living
A Lawrence Kushner Reader Intro. by *Thomas Moore*

Whether you are new to Kushner or a devoted fan, you'll find inspiration here. With samplings from each of Kushner's works, and a generous amount of new material, this book is to be read and reread, each time discovering deeper layers of meaning in our lives.
6 x 9, 240 pp, Quality PB, ISBN 1-58023-042-3 **$16.95**; HC, ISBN 1-58023-014-8 **$23.95**

Because Nothing Looks Like God

by *Lawrence and Karen Kushner*; Full-color illus. by *Dawn W. Majewski*

What is God like? The first collaborative work by husband-and-wife team Lawrence and Karen Kushner introduces children to the possibilities of spiritual life with three poetic spiritual stories. Real-life examples of happiness and sadness—from goodnight stories, to the hope and fear felt the first time at bat, to the closing moments of life—invite us to explore, together with our children, the questions we all have about God, no matter what our age. **For ages 4 & up**
11 x 8½, 32 pp, HC, Full-color illus., ISBN 1-58023-092-X **$16.95**

Invisible Lines of Connection: *Sacred Stories of the Ordinary* **AWARD WINNER!**
6 x 9, 160 pp, Quality PB, ISBN 1-879045-98-2 **$15.95**; HC, ISBN 1-879045-52-4 **$21.95**

Honey from the Rock: *An Introduction to Jewish Mysticism* **SPECIAL ANNIVERSARY EDITION**
6 x 9, 176 pp, Quality PB, ISBN 1-58023-073-3 **$15.95**

The Book of Letters: *A Mystical Hebrew Alphabet* **AWARD WINNER!**
Popular HC Edition, 6 x 9, 80 pp, 2-color text, ISBN 1-879045-00-1 **$24.95**; *Deluxe Gift Edition,* 9 x 12, 80 pp, HC, 2-color text, ornamentation, slipcase, ISBN 1-879045-01-X **$79.95**; *Collector's Limited Edition,* 9 x 12, 80 pp, HC, gold-embossed pages, hand-assembled slipcase. With silkscreened print. Limited to 500 signed and numbered copies, ISBN 1-879045-04-4 **$349.00**

The Book of Words: *Talking Spiritual Life, Living Spiritual Talk* **AWARD WINNER!**
6 x 9, 160 pp, Quality PB, 2-color text, ISBN 1-58023-020-2 **$16.95**;
152 pp, HC, ISBN 1-879045-35-4 **$21.95**

God Was in This Place & I, i Did Not Know
Finding Self, Spirituality and Ultimate Meaning
6 x 9, 192 pp, Quality PB, ISBN 1-879045-33-8 **$16.95**

The River of Light: *Jewish Mystical Awareness* **SPECIAL ANNIVERSARY EDITION**
6 x 9, 192 pp, Quality PB, ISBN 1-58023-096-2 **$16.95**

Spirituality & More

The Jewish Lights Spirituality Handbook
A Guide to Understanding, Exploring & Living a Spiritual Life
Ed. by *Stuart M. Matlins, Editor-in-Chief, Jewish Lights Publishing*

Rich, creative material from over 50 spiritual leaders on every aspect of Jewish spirituality today: prayer, meditation, mysticism, study, rituals, special days, the everyday, and more. 6 x 9, 456 pp, Quality PB, ISBN 1-58023-093-8 **$18.95**; HC, ISBN 1-58023-100-4 **$24.95**

Six Jewish Spiritual Paths: *A Rationalist Looks at Spirituality*
by *Rabbi Rifat Sonsino*

The quest for spirituality is universal, but which path to spirituality is right *for you?* A straightforward, objective discussion of the many ways—each valid and authentic—for seekers to gain a richer spiritual life within Judaism. 6 x 9, 208 pp, HC, ISBN 1-58023-095-4 **$21.95**

Criminal Kabbalah
An Intriguing Anthology of Jewish Mystery & Detective Fiction
Edited by *Lawrence W. Raphael*; Foreword by *Laurie R. King*

Twelve of today's best known mystery authors provide an intriguing collection of new stories sure to enlighten at the same time they entertain. 6 x 9, 256 pp, Quality PB, ISBN 1-58023-109-8 **$16.95**

  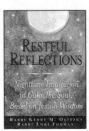  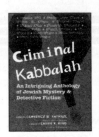

Mystery Midrash: *An Anthology of Jewish Mystery & Detective Fiction* **AWARD WINNER!**
Ed. by Lawrence W. Raphael 6 x 9, 304 pp, Quality PB, ISBN 1-58023-055-5 **$16.95**

Sacred Intentions: *Daily Inspiration to Strengthen the Spirit, Based on Jewish Wisdom*
by Rabbi Kerry M. Olitzky & Rabbi Lori Forman
4½ x 6½, 448 pp, Quality PB, ISBN 1-58023-061-X **$15.95**

Restful Reflections: *Nighttime Inspiration to Calm the Soul, Based on Jewish Wisdom*
by Rabbi Kerry M. Olitzky & Rabbi Lori Forman
4½ x 6½, 448 pp, Quality PB, ISBN 1-58023-091-1 **$15.95**

The Enneagram and Kabbalah: *Reading Your Soul*
by Rabbi Howard A. Addison 6 x 9, 176 pp, Quality PB, ISBN 1-58023-001-6 **$15.95**

Embracing the Covenant: *Converts to Judaism Talk About Why & How*
Ed. and with Intros. by Rabbi Allan L. Berkowitz and Patti Moskovitz
6 x 9, 192 pp, Quality PB, ISBN 1-879045-50-8 **$15.95**

Wandering Stars: *An Anthology of Jewish Fantasy & Science Fiction* Ed. by Jack Dann; Intro. by Isaac Asimov 6 x 9, 272 pp, Quality PB, ISBN 1-58023-005-9 **$16.95**

Israel—A Spiritual Travel Guide **AWARD WINNER!**
A Companion for the Modern Jewish Pilgrim
by Rabbi Lawrence A. Hoffman 4¾ x 10, 256 pp, Quality PB, ISBN 1-879045-56-7 **$18.95**

Women's Spirituality / Ecology

Torah of the Earth: *Exploring 4,000 Years of Ecology in Jewish Thought*
In 2 Volumes Ed. by *Rabbi Arthur Waskow*

Major new resource offering us an invaluable key to understanding the intersection of ecology and Judaism. Leading scholars provide us with a guided tour of ecological thought from four major Jewish viewpoints.
Vol. 1: *Biblical Israel & Rabbinic Judaism,* 6 x 9, 272 pp, Quality PB, ISBN 1-58023-086-5 **$19.95**
Vol. 2: *Zionism & Eco-Judaism,* 6 x 9, 336 pp, Quality PB, ISBN 1-58023-087-3 **$19.95**

Ecology & the Jewish Spirit: *Where Nature & the Sacred Meet* Ed. and with Intros.
by Ellen Bernstein 6 x 9, 288 pp, Quality PB, ISBN 1-58023-082-2 **$16.95**;
HC, ISBN 1-879045-88-5 **$23.95**

The Jewish Gardening Cookbook: *Growing Plants & Cooking for Holidays & Festivals*
by Michael Brown 6 x 9, 224 pp, Illus., Quality PB, ISBN 1-58023-116-0 **$16.95**;
HC, ISBN 1-58023-004-0 **$21.95**

Moonbeams: *A Hadassah Rosh Hodesh Guide*
Ed. by *Carol Diament, Ph.D.*

This hands-on "idea book" focuses on *Rosh Hodesh,* the festival of the new moon, as a source of spiritual growth for Jewish women. A complete sourcebook that will initiate or rejuvenate women's study groups, it is also perfect for women preparing for *bat mitzvah*, or for anyone interested in learning more about *Rosh Hodesh* observance and what it has to offer. 8½ x 11, 240 pp, Quality PB, ISBN 1-58023-099-7 **$20.00**

The Women's Torah Commentary: *New Insights from Women Rabbis on the 54 Weekly Torah Portions* Ed. by *Rabbi Elyse Goldstein*

For the first time, women rabbis provide a commentary on the entire Five Books of Moses. More than 25 years after the first woman was ordained a rabbi in America, these inspiring teachers bring their rich perspectives to bear on the biblical text. In a week-by-week format; a perfect gift for others, or for yourself. 6 x 9, 496 pp, HC, ISBN 1-58023-076-8 **$34.95**

Lifecycles, in Two Volumes AWARD WINNERS!
V. 1: *Jewish Women on Life Passages & Personal Milestones*
Ed. and with Intros. by Rabbi Debra Orenstein
V. 2: *Jewish Women on Biblical Themes in Contemporary Life*
Ed. and with Intros. by Rabbi Debra Orenstein and Rabbi Jane Rachel Litman
V. 1: 6 x 9, 480 pp, Quality PB, ISBN 1-58023-018-0 **$19.95**; HC, ISBN 1-879045-14-1 **$24.95**
V. 2: 6 x 9, 464 pp, Quality PB, ISBN 1-58023-019-9 **$19.95**

ReVisions: *Seeing Torah through a Feminist Lens* AWARD WINNER!
by Rabbi Elyse Goldstein 5½ x 8½, 224 pp, Quality PB, ISBN 1-58023-117-9 **$16.95**;
208 pp, HC, ISBN 1-58023-047-4 **$19.95**

The Year Mom Got Religion: *One Woman's Midlife Journey into Judaism*
by Lee Meyerhoff Hendler 6 x 9, 208 pp, Quality PB, ISBN 1-58023-070-9 **$15.95**

Spirituality

Does the Soul Survive?
A Jewish Journey to Belief in Afterlife, Past Lives & Living with Purpose
by *Rabbi Elie Kaplan Spitz*; Foreword by *Brian L. Weiss, M.D.*

Spitz relates his own experiences and those shared with him by people he has worked with as a rabbi, and shows us that belief in afterlife and past lives, so often approached with reluctance, is in fact true to Jewish tradition. 6 x 9, 288 pp, HC, ISBN 1-58023-094-6 **$21.95**

The Women's Torah Commentary: *New Insights from Women Rabbis*
on the 54 Weekly Torah Portions Ed. by *Rabbi Elyse Goldstein*

For the first time, women rabbis provide a commentary on the entire Torah. In a week-by-week format; a perfect gift for others, or for yourself.
6 x 9, 496 pp, HC, ISBN 1-58023-076-8 **$34.95**

The Gift of Kabbalah
Discovering the Secrets of Heaven, Renewing Your Life on Earth
by *Tamar Frankiel, Ph.D.*

Makes accessible the mysteries of Kabbalah. Traces Kabbalah's evolution in Judaism and shows us its most important gift: a way of revealing the connection between our "everyday" life and the spiritual oneness of the universe. 6 x 9, 256 pp, HC, ISBN 1-58023-108-X **$21.95**

 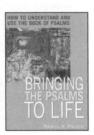   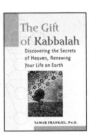

Bringing the Psalms to Life: *How to Understand and Use the Book of Psalms*
by Rabbi Daniel F. Polish 6 x 9, 208 pp, Quality PB, ISBN 1-58023-157-8 **$16.95**;
HC, ISBN 1-58023-077-6 **$21.95**

The Empty Chair: *Finding Hope and Joy—*
Timeless Wisdom from a Hasidic Master, Rebbe Nachman of Breslov **AWARD WINNER!**
4 x 6, 128 pp, Deluxe PB, 2-color text, ISBN 1-879045-67-2 **$9.95**

The Gentle Weapon: *Prayers for Everyday and Not-So-Everyday Moments*
Adapted from the Wisdom of Rebbe Nachman of Breslov
4 x 6, 144 pp, Deluxe PB, 2-color text, ISBN 1-58023-022-9 **$9.95**

Ancient Secrets: *Using the Stories of the Bible to Improve Our Everyday Lives*
by Rabbi Levi Meier, Ph.D. 5½ x 8½, 288 pp, Quality PB, ISBN 1-58023-064-4 **$16.95**

Or phone, fax, mail or e-mail to: **JEWISH LIGHTS Publishing**
Sunset Farm Offices, Route 4 • P.O. Box 237 • Woodstock, Vermont 05091
Tel: (802) 457-4000 • Fax: (802) 457-4004 • www.jewishlights.com
Credit card orders: **(800) 962-4544** (9AM–5PM ET Monday–Friday)
Generous discounts on quantity orders. SATISFACTION GUARANTEED. Prices subject to change.